How to Own the Room

www.penguin.co.uk

HOW TO OWN THE ROOM

Women and the Art of Brilliant Speaking

VIV GROSKOP

BANTAM PRESS

TRANSWORLD PUBLISHERS
Penguin Random House, One Embassy Gardens,
8 Viaduct Gardens, London SW11 7BW
www.penguin.co.uk

Transworld is part of the Penguin Random House group of companies
whose addresses can be found at global.penguinrandomhouse.com

Penguin
Random House
UK

First published in Great Britain in 2018 by Bantam Press
an imprint of Transworld Publishers
Revised editions published in 2020 and 2022

A CIP catalogue record for this book
is available from the British Library.

ISBN 9781787631120

Typeset in 10.25/15pt Avenir LT Pro by Jouve (UK), Milton Keynes
Printed and bound in Great Britain by Clays Ltd, Elcograf S.p.A.

The authorized representative in the EEA is Penguin Random House
Ireland, Morrison Chambers, 32 Nassau Street, Dublin D02 YH68.

Penguin Random House is committed to a sustainable
future for our business, our readers and our planet. This book
is made from Forest Stewardship Council® certified paper.

For the three most brilliant women in my life:
Anna, Trudy and Vera

CONTENTS

INTRODUCTION

Welcome to the re-issue of *How to Own the Room*, a book which helps women to find their voice, manage their nerves and work out their own 'room-owning' style. Even if they think they don't have a room-owning style. In fact, *especially* if they think they don't have a room-owning style.

Since the book was first published in 2018, I have read thousands of messages, reviews and social-media posts from women who have done the following as a result of *How to Own the Room*: aced job interviews; applied for positions they previously thought they weren't capable of; felt more confident in awkward situations; given high-pressure keynote speeches; given thank-you speeches at birthdays and 'best woman' speeches at weddings; taken creative risks on stage and on the page; said 'yes' to conferences and panels as well as radio, TV and podcast appearances; become more confident in their teaching; won contracts and deals; secured investment, promotions and pay rises; performed one-woman shows from scratch; had difficult conversations with bosses, colleagues, clients, friends, partners, children; been more active and open on social media; and even complained about bad service in restaurants (one major room-owning challenge I'm still working on).

INTRODUCTION

Meanwhile, in that time, the way we perceive women in public life in their 'room-owning' moments has travelled to a whole new level. The influence of speakers who are under the age of thirty-five (in fact, often under the age of twenty) has grown at speed – from campaigners like Malala Yousafzai and Greta Thunberg to politicians like Alexandria Ocasio-Cortez in the US and Zarah Sultana in the UK. This was a trend I could see was emerging fast as I was writing the book and I underlined it as strongly as I could in its pages. But I had no idea quite how rapidly it would take hold. For a long time during the twentieth century there was a perception that 'brilliant speaking' was the preserve of older, senior people – usually men – with established status or in elected office. That is absolutely no longer the case.

This radical shift, in the space of a few short years, is incredibly inspiring. One of the key messages of this book is that in the twenty-first century we do not know what power looks like until we see it. The qualities of confidence and authority have a different face – and a different voice – compared with our previous ideas of what power and leadership 'should' look and sound like. That change has advanced in a way I didn't even dare hope for. And it's thrilling.

In this new era, you have an opportunity to present yourself in a way that feels authentic and impactful to you, without having to match up to some mythical pre-existing standard. Of course, there are some basic rules of thumb, which I cover in depth in the book, that will always apply to speaking up and speaking out successfully: eye contact, humility, generosity, clarity and authenticity are not going to go out of fashion any time soon.

But while the very basics stay in place, increasingly audiences – both online and in person – are fascinated by what they haven't seen before, by different kinds of communication, by what's new, exciting, dynamic and fresh, by what feels real and what feels urgent. However you express that – in your body language, in your choice of words, in your energy – is up to you. The joy is that you do not need a personality transplant. As a speaker you might be neurodivergent, you might be introverted, you might be allergic to the idea of being some fake version of 'charismatic', or you might simply be someone who is softly spoken . . . These are all qualities you can use to help you own the room. And the more we see of different kinds of speakers, the more we realize – with a sigh of relief – that none of us have to pretend to be something we're not. Again, that is a change that is moving even more quickly than I expected. The idea that you have to do and say certain things to be a 'good public speaker', or that you need to look a certain way or follow convention, is being swiftly eroded. Any sense of 'should' in this arena is increasingly redundant. Old ideas that you 'should' sound a certain way, that you 'should' have a particular accent, dress a particular way or construct a speech in a set pattern, are increasingly being proven to be outdated.

Has the global pandemic accelerated this shift? Definitely. Not least because our preconceptions about 'presence' have been completely upended in a world where the room might well be a virtual one. Now we have all had to work out how to do the equivalent of standing up and talking to the group from our webcam or phone screen. Plus, if you are looking to build your own audience, you are just as likely to do that remotely – on TikTok, LinkedIn, Instagram Stories, YouTube, or whatever your latest platform of choice is – as you are to find a platform through face-to-face networking. This is wonderful news, as it means that you can mould things the way you want to. But that universal access is also incredibly daunting, because the field is wide open and the choices available to you can feel bewildering. That's where this book comes in: the tips, tricks and food for thought that I lay out here are all designed to foster a belief that you can do this the way you want to. All you need is confidence and a plan.

During the months of lockdown, when many companies and networks across the world were able to communicate only via screens from our own domestic spaces, our idea of what professionalism looks like became a lot less prescriptive. Thank goodness. The gap between our professional and personal personae collapsed in many industries and there has been a move towards informality, 'keeping it real' and perhaps even a kind of intimacy. (There is something very intimate about seeing colleagues in their domestic space, something that would have been unimaginable even ten years ago.) Again, I see this as a good thing. Because it means you get to own the room – or the Zoom – by being yourself, without having to pretend to be something or someone you're not. But it also allows for confusion and insecurity. How do you know what the boundaries are? How do you know whether you're being too relaxed? How can you be taken seriously in an informal setting like your kitchen? I explore some of these ideas in the new, inevitable post-pandemic chapter 'How to Own the Zoom'.

Maybe the biggest and most unexpected shift since this book was first published has been inside me personally. In 2018, I wanted to write about women's speaker styles, confidence and performance excellence simply because there was very little material on this topic. And because they say you should always write the book that you would most want to read. But once the book came out and the 'How to Own the Room' podcast took off, where I've been able to tap into the wisdom and advice of an amazing guestlist of women, I realized – with a gulp of sudden anxiety – that there is a vast, gaping chasm of unmet need around the topic of women and confidence. Over the course of hundreds of events, both face-to-face and on-line, I have been reminded time and again of the hunger for information, insight, analysis, support, reassurance and cheer-leading; for a place to swap war stories; for a place to learn and pick up practical tips and hacks. In one sense, that discovery was great news, of course, because the book and the interviews on the 'How to Own the Room' podcast are all designed to meet those needs. But it also made me incredibly sad. There are still many of us – too many of us – who are questioning ourselves and wondering if we're good enough to express ourselves, to speak up, to say what we really want to say. There is so much agonizing over whether it's even OK to think that you can own the room, and that's before you've worked out how you're going to do it. If you identify with that – and I haven't met many women who don't – then let this be the last moment when you give in to those doubts.

What I hope this book does, more than anything, is imbue you with a feeling of such confidence that you are emboldened to find your own version of owning the room without someone else telling you what that looks like. The main aim of this book is to give you the internal and external tools for you to shine in the spotlight, speak up whenever you want to or need to, and hold your own, on your own terms and without having to worry about anyone else's opinion, including mine. Enjoy!

Viv Groskop
March 2022

1

The Art of Brilliant Speaking: What Does It Mean to Own the Room?

Anyone can speak.
But you have to want to

A woman's preaching is like a dog's walking on
its hind legs – it's not done well; but you're
surprised to find it's done at all.

Samuel Johnson

Women don't need to find a voice. They have a
voice. They need to feel empowered to use it and
people need to be encouraged to listen.

Meghan Markle

There is a wonderful scene with Meryl Streep in *The
Post*. She plays Katherine Graham, the first female pub-
lisher of a major American newspaper. It's 1963 and Graham
is an uneasy leader of a business with revenues of $84
million. She has inherited the newspaper from her late husband, who in turn inherited it from Graham's father.
Everyone knows that she is running a company her father
didn't want her to run. And she's only running it because
her husband is dead. Next time you have a crisis at work,
think about how she must have felt, wafting around her

mansion in a Halston kaftan, wondering how she was ever going to get anyone to take her seriously. This, my friends, is a leadership challenge.

As the film begins, the company is facing a crisis and needs to raise cash urgently. Privately, and especially in moments of solitude, Graham is cool, calm and collected. She knows what she wants to happen and has rehearsed a plan. All she has to do is convince the board, which consists of her and about twenty men. She's ready. She's armed with all the facts. Except in the meeting she can't get the words out. She knows exactly what she wants to say. She even has it written down in a notebook in front of her. She has memorized every statistic, every financial detail, every argument. But nothing will come out of her mouth at the crucial moment. Instead she has to listen to a man parroting the exact words she has prepared while she sits there mute, unable to say the one thing that would make a difference: 'Wait. I would like to speak.' Yes, she owns the company. But when it counts, she cannot own the room.

How many of us have experienced that moment, even without the Halston maxi-dress and multi-million-dollar newspaper company? We all know what that feels like, the split second when words fail us and we know we've lost the opportunity.

There are lots of books on the great art of speech-making. They tend to focus on 'what to say in your speech'.

They don't tell you what to do when nothing will come out of your mouth. And they don't tell you how to get over the general anxiety about speaking that most people very naturally have. They don't tell you what to do in the moments you're made, as a woman, to feel small. They don't tell you how to own the room.

Instead these books will warn you not to make a joke at the beginning of a speech because your audience will think the whole thing is stand-up comedy. (I think it's fine to take a risk.) They will teach you rhetorical devices on how to group ideas in threes because that's easier to remember and easier for the audience to focus on. (This is good advice.) And they will tell you to use quotes from well-known figures to punctuate your thoughts or illustrate a conclusion. (This is not bad advice. Also: see how in this last paragraph I've just made three points? That's a good structure to follow in speeches. Three things in succession is pleasing.)

We all know, though, that this kind of advice is for Cloud Cuckoo Land. There is no point in knowing what you're going to say in this fictitious brilliant speech if you're too nervous to make it in the first place. This is really advice for people who are never actually going to give a speech: they just want to fantasize about what it would be like if they *did*. Oh, the amazing things they would say! Oh, the rhetorical flourishes they would add! Oh, how the crowd would marvel and sigh! It's exactly like Meryl Streep as

Katherine Graham in that scene. She would have given them a piece of her mind, those boardroom men! She would have wowed them with her plan! She would have aced it! Yes. Except she didn't. And she couldn't. Why not? Because, I would argue, she didn't want to do it badly enough to let go of her nerves and leap.

What the traditional advice does not focus on is (a) how to get yourself into the frame of mind where you think you actually can give a speech in reality and not just in your imagination, and (b) how to make that speech happen, while accepting that nerves and anxiety are a part of life. In this book, we're going to focus not on the speech itself but on you as a speaker. Who do you want to emulate? Who inspires you? How can you channel that person? How can you get a piece of what they've got? What do they do that makes them so good? To be the speaker you want to be is much more important than the actual speech. Because without your own belief that you can own the room – and your desire to own it – the room is already lost.

Form matters more than content

Too often when we discuss public speaking, we talk about the content. What exactly did the speaker say that made this particular speech so memorable? How did they phrase that fantastic quote just so? How did they make those points so succinctly and cleverly? This is all well and good. And we should analyse brilliant speeches for their content. Whenever a memorable speech pops up, particularly one that resonates for decades, someone generally spent a long time writing it. But when I'm talking to people in presentation workshops – especially, I have to say, women – they are not worried about the content of their speech. They are worried about talking in public. How should they stand? Where should they look? What if they're nervous? What if they should have recommended someone else to give the speech? What if, like Katherine Graham, they bottle it at the last moment?

We are right to have these anxieties as we know the truth about speaking. Just as anyone who has ever been on television knows the truth about television. No one who sees you on television cares about the clever (or incredibly stupid) things you say: they are much more interested in what you were wearing and how relaxed you looked. Please learn from my painful example and never go on Sky News wearing a too-tight leopard-print sweater that strains over your bosom. For indeed, whether we like it or not, we human beings are visual creatures and we love 'reading' others (fun and low effort) much more than concentrating on the words they're speaking (boring and hard work). We all know that we could have the most blisteringly brilliant speech of all time written by Jane Austen, with contributions from Charles Dickens and edited by the TED committee. But unless we look the part in our gestures, our attitude and how we carry ourselves, no one will listen to a goddamn word of it. The more we can master the 'fun' part (how we come across), the more likely people are to focus on the 'boring' part (our message).

There was a famous study in 1971 by Professor Albert Mehrabian, psychologist and communications theorist. He concluded that 93 per cent of communication is non-verbal. Only seven per cent is based on the content of our speech. Of the non-verbal communication, 55 per cent was body language, 38 per cent tone of voice. While this study has since been the subject of heated debate, one thing seems clear to me: his conclusion is that when we are communicating, 'meaning' and 'words' are two distinct things. We infer a lot of meaning from the bits of our communications that are not words: tone of voice, facial expression, body language.

Psychologists now accept that around 60 to 90 per cent of our communication is likely to be non-verbal. This makes sense to me. If you watch a film with the sound turned off, you have a pretty good idea of the meaning without hearing any of the words. You can watch a couple on an opposite train platform and know whether they're happy together. You can see a politician on a screen and know instantly, before they have spoken, whether you trust them or not. You can witness a woman in an undersized animal-print top and feel pity for her. We're trained to read emotions, facial expressions, body language and tone long before we understand words.

That doesn't mean the text of a speech is insignificant. Of course the text is important. And many great speeches come from way before the era of video and have survived and resonated across the years, without any non-verbal communication or physical evidence of how they were delivered. So I am not saying these speeches are redundant. What I am saying is that this is not a book about how to write a great speech. It is a book about how to be powerful in your speaking. That is not the same thing. It's more about the sort of person you need to be to give your speaking a fighting chance. And how, like Katherine Graham eventually did, to look and feel like that person the second you walk into the room.

'Hang on a minute. What makes you think women need help? Are you saying they're incompetent? And what about men?'

Let's get the 'woman' thing out of the way. Yes, this is a book for women. No, there is never going to be a book called *How to Own the Room: Men and the Art of Brilliant Speaking*. Unless maybe Fathers 4 Justice rise up and decide to publish it because they feel discriminated against. Also, guess what? Almost all the books ever written about public speaking and rhetoric have been about men, by men and for men. Surprise, surprise. We all know the inequalities that women have faced, and that for centuries there was opposition to women being heard. We all know that cultural norms and social conditioning cause some women to impose limitations on themselves and be overly self-critical. No sensible person would dispute any of this. I've felt such pressure myself. Few women haven't.

There is also an increasing amount of research analysing these social trends, which are often unconscious or subconscious. Which is great. There are studies about interrupting and about mansplaining. (During the presidential debate in 2016, Donald Trump interrupted Hillary Clinton fifty-one times. She interrupted him seventeen times.) There are endless debates and discussions about how much of this is 'nature' and how much 'nurture'. This is all to the good, as the more we understand about these things, the better.

However. One of the most important things about speaking is honing things. So I make no apologies for having a single-minded focus in this book: on you as a speaker. And not on the culture surrounding you. Whenever I teach speaking and presentation in a corporate context to all-female groups, the first thing I say is: 'We are not here to moan about how others behave. We are here to focus on how you behave.' (I also teach mixed groups, by the way, and have seen men cry in these sessions many times.

Women don't have the monopoly on insecurity.) Of course, there is a time and place to examine structural inequalities, to campaign and to demand changes to the law, but there should also be a time and place to think about you. And this book is it. This is a space for you to think about your strengths and how you can build on them. And to think about how you can amplify your voice.

I don't pretend for a second that this stuff is easy. It's undeniable that traditionally there have been fewer speaking opportunities for women. In her speech 'We Should All Be Feminists', Chimamanda Ngozi Adichie quotes the environmentalist and Kenyan Nobel Prize-winner Wangari Maathai: 'The higher you go, the fewer women there are.' That is neither inaccurate nor controversial: it describes most industries and power structures anywhere in the world over the past fifty years. But my mission here is not to diagnose the problem. Instead, it's to encourage women to focus their efforts, create their own opportunities and feel great about their ability to communicate. There will be some tough love. But as Oprah Winfrey says: 'There is no discrimination against excellence.'

As Adichie suggests in her speech, the status quo is, to some extent, a numbers problem. There are fewer women in senior roles in most professions and it's in those roles that we are most likely to see and hear women speak. Or, at least, that's how it has been until very recently. The difficulties this causes seem to affect even the most unlikely of women. This is Amal Clooney: 'I remember all the stages in my career where I almost didn't have enough confidence to try for something, almost didn't have the guts to follow something I was excited about doing, because I didn't know anyone else who'd done it, or other people made me question it.'

As Adichie goes on to say, things are changing. A thousand years ago, we lived in a world where physical strength dictated leadership and our bias was towards believing that men were 'the strong ones'. Now, argues Adichie, we live in complex and fast-moving times full of uncertainty. This is a good thing and a bad thing. Whatever happens, it is certain to create opportunity for some, perhaps not those who have traditionally been leaders. Leadership no longer necessarily comes from strength – let alone physical strength. It comes instead from those who are more intelligent, more creative, more innovative: 'And there are no hormones for those attributes,' says Adichie. As human beings we are slow to accept this, she adds, because we see that we have evolved, 'But our ideas of gender have not evolved.'

With her help, though, and with the help of others, they are evolving. And maybe not as slowly as it sometimes seems. Two of the most impressive speakers of recent years are women under the age of twenty-five and not from traditional power structures: Malala Yousafzai (for her Nobel Peace Prize speech in 2014) and Ariana Grande (for her speech at the One Love Manchester benefit concert in 2017). I notice that a lot of younger women are less constrained by the stereotypes that have plagued those of us who are older. They seem to have fewer hang-ups about speaking. This is the sort of evolution that might cheer Chimamanda Ngozi Adichie.

It has never been easier to find opportunities to own the room

The situations you could choose to imagine where you might challenge some of the old stereotypes and show how you 'own the room' are up to you. You may want to get to TED Talk level. You may want to behave with more calm and precision in presentations. You may want to get a word in edgeways at meetings. You may wish your voice quaked a little less during stressful phone calls. Or you may just want to look a bit less of a numpty when appearing on the small screen that is your mobile telephone. Or perhaps you have been completely avoiding all kinds of small-screen interaction because you are afraid of coming across as a numpty. Join the club.

It's time for us to get over this. Avoiding the small screen is like shutting yourself in a room and never looking in a mirror because you're afraid of your own reflection.

There has never been a better time to learn how to control the way you present yourself to the world. Because there are so many opportunities to show who you are. Even as little as a decade ago you might have had to wait to be chosen to speak, whether it was in the debating team or as a TV presenter. Now you can set up your own TV channel with a couple of clicks of the mouse. You can host a podcast, launch a vlog, broadcast live from your keyboard right now. You can send an email in the next five minutes to propose a TEDx Talk. Not only are you able to push yourself forward in a way that has never been possible before, but also it's almost expected of us all.

With these opportunities comes pressure. For a long time, being a good speaker has been regarded as a positive asset or a way of gaining an advantage over the competition. Now it's a necessity. It's increasingly difficult for anyone to avoid broadcast-standard communication, however much they may hate it. I don't think these things are inherently more challenging for women than they are for men, but we still don't have many prominent female role models in leadership and public life, which can make some women understandably hesitant about speaking up. It's hard to know what a form of behaviour will look like in you when you haven't seen anything similar in someone like you. I hope this book will be the first step to not caring too much about that any more and just finding out what it looks like for you anyway. If you have to be the first person who looks and sounds like you, so what? Own it. Be the first.

The limits and benefits of trying to be like Michelle Obama

YouTube and TED are incredibly useful to anyone who wants to study the art of brilliant speaking. We are now able to see excellent speaking up close and watch a speech as many times as we want. In years gone by it was only the text of a speech that would live on (because there was no video footage of it), which is why, historically, most studies of public speaking concentrate on what to say rather than how you say it.

The disadvantage, though, in the ready availability of great speeches is that we may compare ourselves to the impossible. It's easy to forget that in the situations where Michelle Obama and TED Talkers are presenting, the speakers often have access to speech writers, voice coaches, notes and autocue. There is often a whole support system behind them. Just as it would be wrong to compare your hair, make-up and grooming with the standard in a Beyoncé video, these speeches are often the airbrushed equivalent. Lots of women say, 'If I was going to be a speaker, I'd want to speak like Michelle Obama.' But if you had Michelle Obama's support system, you probably would be able to speak like Michelle Obama very easily. Without her back-up team, the rest of us are going to have to work a little bit harder.

That said, the bar for speaking is often set far lower

than we think, and a lot of TED Talks (and footage from commencement speeches, or corporate and political events) show this. Sometimes it's reassuring to realize that you don't actually have to be that good. One of the biggest aspects of successful communication in any setting, whether it's getting the outcome you want from a phone call or blowing away everyone in your office with a fantastic end-of-year thank-you speech, is managing your own expectations. You are not going to be Bette Davis in *All About Eve* on your phone call. And you don't need to be. You are not going to be Oprah Winfrey on *Super Soul Sundays* when you've just drawn the raffle for the office Secret Santa. And you don't need to be. All you need to be is a credible, honest version of yourself. And that in itself will be better than being Bette or Oprah because it will be real. (Obviously Bette Davis and Oprah should not try to be you. That would be wrong.)

So-called formal public-speaking engagements are thin on the ground nowadays, thank goodness, as most of them were awful. Let's be honest, who has ever really wanted to be involved in 'public speaking'? Except, perhaps, an over-excited prefect at Eton in 1953. The idea of 'public speaking' is outdated, a discipline taught forty years ago when anyone who could string a sentence together would be picked out to join some awful 'debating team'. You would have to prepare some godawful sermon beginning 'This house believes . . .' and ending with something like '. . . the monarchy should be abolished' or '. . . pigeons are grossly misunderstood and are not really vermin.' ('Rats with Wings' was a real speech by a girl I went to school with. It won a debating competition.)

What a complete waste of time all that was. This house believes that the old-school kind of preparation for public speaking is enough to put you off speaking in public ever again. Motion carried.

Not everyone wants to be an evangelical preacher or a stand-up comedian or a motivational speaker. In fact, for most people these things are their idea of a total nightmare. (And rightly so, I can report, as someone who has done at least two of those things.) But increasingly we are expected to bring a flavour of these professions into our everyday working lives. Also, with the advent of digital technology, if you have a message you want to spread you have to amplify your voice and get your words out there. Otherwise one of your competitors will beat you to it. This is not a time to be quiet, keep your head down and hope that someone might hear your modest, interesting whisper.

It goes without saying that the ability to speak up, speak out and be heard is also crucial in the wake of #MeToo and #TimesUp. These are fledgling social-justice movements. It doesn't seem outlandish to suggest that they could receive a considerable backlash in the coming years, whether that takes the form of women being told to

'Shut up because we've heard enough about this now', or it slips off the agenda because the news cycle moves on and people get bored. Women need to be ready to counter both those eventualities.

It is human to find public speaking difficult: the struggle is not personal to you

If I could have one wish for my daughter, who will soon be going into her teens, it would be that she is able to speak her mind wherever, whenever and however she wants. And to do that with the confidence that she can make herself heard. Note my wording: that I want her to be heard. Not that I want her to be listened to. Although, of course, I do want that. But I know that is never a given. A really useful gift in life is the ability to make yourself heard, whether others want to listen to you or not. Power is not given, it is taken. Attention is not given, it is taken. To know how to take these things when you want them is a lifelong skill.

I would also wish for her to accept nerves and anxiety, and work with them. When those things are present in us, they are simply a sign that we are functioning human beings. They are not a sign that (a) we should not be doing this or (b) public speaking is intrinsically terrifying. But the sad fact is that most people's dream is not to deliver a speech that is as amazing as Oprah Winfrey's at the Golden Globes. It is not even to deliver a good speech. Most people's dream is *not to be nervous about public speaking*. And this is a false and crazy dream. In fact, it's such a crazy dream that we're all more likely to win a Golden Globe for Lifetime Achievement than we are to stop being nervous about public speaking.

You can't get around fear. You can only go through it. And the way to go through it is to speak in public and get more used to it. It helps to remember that even the most confident people on the planet can be nervous about their speaking. Take, for example, Bishop Michael Curry, the charismatic preacher who spoke at Prince Harry and Meghan Markle's wedding for double the length of time he was supposed to. Would you imagine he is ever nervous about anything? He doesn't seem like a shy, retiring type. I mean, he had enough of a sense of entitlement and self-belief to overrun at an event that was being televised in front of a global audience of 50 million. (To give a sense of proportion, four years later I'm still beating myself up for overrunning by thirty seconds on a ten-minute comedy set at a smelly basement club in front of an audience of fifteen people. Some of us outstay our welcome on stage more easily than others.) However, Bishop Curry said afterwards that he was riddled with nerves and often is before a performance like that. His tip? Get in the moment. Focus on what's in front of you. Think of something outside yourself. 'Even if I was somewhat nervous . . . [my task was] to zero in and focus on the couple and what God's love might mean for them at this moment.' Next time you feel nervous, think: Me and the preacher, both.

The main factors influencing successful public speaking are these: commitment, practice and guts. If you really want to speak up, no one is stopping you. Except, of course, yourself. I've lost count of the number of women who have told me they've turned down invitations to speak on panels or give a keynote or take part in a media appearance on television or radio because they 'didn't feel ready' or they 'might look stupid' or because 'I'm sure they could find someone better'. Over the years I've spoken to dozens of journalists, TV and radio producers who make calls to women all the time and hear these excuses.

And, I'm sorry, they are excuses. It's anecdotal but these people will tell you that men generally do not respond in the same way. That's not to say that no man has ever turned down a speaking appearance because he was nervous. But in general men are less likely to doubt why their expertise has been sought. They take the call or make the appearance if it benefits them. Or they turn it down politely if it doesn't. They don't angst over it. Women do. This is about one thing: guts.

I'm not judging or criticizing this reaction because I do the same thing, even though I'm constantly vigilant about it. Only recently I turned down a radio series and recommended a male colleague instead because I thought he was better suited for it. In theory I was right. In reality I gave away a (paid) job to a man. When the producer sent me a recording of the series to say thank you (for the broadcast I had generously helped create for no monetary reward and which did not feature me), I could have stuck pins in my eyes. That's just one opportunity I cheated myself of both financially and creatively. We've all done it. We all continue to do it. We count ourselves out even when others are trying to count us in. It's time to start avoiding this where possible, without expecting to judge it perfectly right every time.

Sometimes I think these producers or organizers have a responsibility to twist women's arms and call them on their excuses. But the fact is, we're not babies and we have to learn to say yes and be ready, even if we think we're not. It is not the world's job to cajole us into these things. If we wait for encouragement and enthusiasm, we will be waiting a very long time. We need to have more confidence that, by saying yes more often, we'll improve if we need to. Not that we may need to. And it's not right to give all these opportunities to the show-offs and extroverts, who are desperate to take them. (Although, I put my hands up, I'm pretty much one of them most of the time.)

As Susan Cain, TED speaker and author of *Quiet: The Power of Introverts in a World that Can't Stop Talking*, puts it: 'There is zero correlation between being the best talker and having the best ideas.' Let yourself put your ideas forward even if, right now, you don't think you're the best talker. The more you talk about your ideas publicly, the better they will sound.

There are exceptions to this rule, naturally. I'm not a fan of women being included arbitrarily or to tick a box. There have been occasions when I've known that's the reason I've been asked to an event, especially when it's talking about an area I genuinely know very little about. I once turned down a serious visual-arts discussion for which I was objectively ill-suited because I felt that a visual artist or an academic should be featured instead of me. The organizers were angry and said, 'But you of all people should support the idea of women being on a panel.' I agreed in principle. But I only support women being featured when they'll be shown in their best light. And I would have been way out of my depth. The more you say yes to things, the more you know in your gut when something is really not right for you.

Saying yes to speaking opportunities (and creating them for yourself) has been called 'inoculation training'. The more you do it, the more you protect yourself, the less affected you are by 'dis-ease'. Susan Cain has said that she spent a year 'practising public speaking every chance I got' in the run-up to the publication of her book, which was accompanied by her TED Talk. She's very aware of the painful irony of giving speeches about what it's like to be introverted. Her message is: If I can do it, anyone can. We hear you, Susan.

Tips and Tricks

There are some elemental physical rules I tend to adhere to if I'm teaching a class (of men and women) about speaking. They are the absolute basics to remember before any speaking moment when you're standing up and talking to others, whether it's to one person or to two thousand. They are also a great reminder of how to relax if you have a sudden attack of nerves.

— Shoulders back. Chest forward. Plant your feet hip-width apart and rest the weight of your body evenly across the soles of your feet. Not only does this look relaxed and neutral but the effort involved in doing it also makes you forget about your speech and distracts you for a moment. That's a good thing. Before any speech, send your thoughts and energy to your feet to calm your nerves and restore yourself to this moment (instead of your brain racing ahead into the future and a great big flashing neon sign marked 'Failure' and/or 'Everyone hates you'). Can you feel your feet rooted to the floor? This is why people talk about feeling 'grounded'. It always reads well to an audience if you look grounded or anchored.

— Monitor your breathing. A lot of people's anxiety around speaking can be fixed just by getting them to remember to breathe, smile and pause. There will always be adrenalin around when you're in front of a group of people, but exposing yourself to it more often and learning to breathe through it allows you to stay relaxed and focused.

— Let your brain drop into your stomach. (I know that sounds odd. Just close your eyes and imagine it. It's a way of centring yourself and switching off from all the thoughts in your head.) You can do this just before you go on stage or start a speech. Or you can remember it while you're speaking. Really try to feel it happening. I find it useful because it gets me out of the anxiety in my head and reminds me to just be. All you're doing when you're speaking is being a human saying words in front of other humans. Why is that such a big deal? Put your brain in your stomach and say the words.

— Breathe through the soles of your feet. This is a great way to get focused on your breathing and be connected to your entire body. Imagine you have nostrils in the soles of your feet. You breathe through them instead of breathing through your nose. (Yes, I know, this is mad, too. Just go with it.) Imagine drawing the breath up through your entire body and breathing it back out through your feet. This also works really well for insomnia, by the way.

Quick fix? Think: Shoulders back. Breathe. Brain in stomach. Breathe through feet.

Exercises

— Give yourself ten minutes to sit down and make notes (a) in answer to these questions and (b) about what comes up for you emotionally when you think about them.

— What excuses are you making to yourself about your speaking? What excuses are you making not to find speaker opportunities? Write it all down.

— What are your limiting beliefs about your speaking? Make a list of all the things you believe are holding you back (i.e. 'I don't have a strong voice'; 'I wouldn't know what to say'; 'There are no opportunities at my work-place.') Write them down. Spell them out. Admit them to yourself.

— What is your negative inner monologue? What does your inner critic sound like? Your inner monologue is what you say to yourself all day long. It's worth checking in to see if you're feeding yourself unhelpful mes-sages. ('You're not the kind of person who would ever be able to give a speech'; 'Why are you even reading this book?'; 'The idea of you speaking is just ridiculous.') This is not common sense talking. It's the inner critic. The inner critic can poison all good intentions and stop us in our tracks. If everyone listened to their inner critic, nothing good would ever happen. Write down – without judgement, for now – ten things your inner critic is telling you.

— Sit with these ideas for a few days and see what's true for you. Then go back to the list of limiting beliefs. Next to each statement write an opposite truth. Beside 'I don't have a strong voice', write 'I can work on strengthening my voice' or 'I don't have the weakest voice' or 'I don't need a strong voice because microphones have been invented.' For 'I don't know what to say', try 'I can work on speech ideas in advance' or 'Friends or colleagues will have advice on what they'd ideally like to hear me talking about.' And next to 'There are no opportunities at my workplace', put something like 'I could create opportunities at work myself'; 'I can create opportunities outside work'; 'I could look for a new job.'

— Then look at your list of things that the inner critic says to you. US coach Tara Mohr focuses intensively on working with this voice, revealing it, then ridiculing it. If you sense you have a voice like this, giving you unhelpful feedback, then try imagining it with a funny cartoon voice, like Bugs Bunny's or Daffy Duck's. Is it really good advice from yourself that you're listening to? Or is it just nonsense?

2

Be More Michelle: Inside the World of Happy High Status (also starring George Clooney and the Fly-catcher)

Don't be afraid of your own power

When I first heard about the concept of 'happy high status' – the inner quality that is essential for an electric public-speaking performance – it was described to me like this. Imagine George Clooney is at a Hollywood cocktail party. He is wearing black tie because everyone at the party is wearing black tie. It's that kind of party. A guest arrives. He is especially excited to be there. He spots a group of friends and sets off across the room to join them. On the way he resolves to pick up a drink. You can guess what's coming. Distracted, the guest taps a waiter on the shoulder and asks for a cocktail. The 'waiter', of course, is George Clooney. Faced with a split-second choice between compliance and confrontation, George Clooney waltzes gracefully over to a real waiter with a tray of drinks, picks up a cocktail and hands it to the guest, smiling and entirely unruffled. That is happy high status.

It doesn't matter whether this ever really happened, although I like to think it did. But if it didn't, I will definitely try to enact it when I next see George Clooney at a cocktail party. (I'm sure this will be soon.) And it doesn't matter about the reaction of the guest afterwards who, presumably, in the moment that George Clooney handed him the cocktail must have realized his mistake and had immediately to be taken to the ER. (Ironically enough.) No, what matters is this: the reaction of George Clooney. His status is so high and he is so happy in himself that he's totally fine with someone (a) not recognizing him and (b) taking him for a waiter. He's so fine with it that he will just go and get the cocktail. That is what it is to be happy high status.

Who wouldn't want to be that person? Yes, this is a story about a male person, George Clooney. (And, let's be honest, a lot of good stories are going to feature George Clooney.) But the first thing I thought when I heard it was: This is absolutely what Michelle Obama would do. It's also, to be fair, probably what Barack Obama would do too. But if we're talking about women, it's Michelle Obama who most fully and obviously embodies the idea of happy high status. If you could tell this cocktail story about a woman, Michelle could easily be in the Clooney role. The fact is, this story wouldn't work with a woman because women tend not to wear outfits to cocktail parties that get them mistaken for the staff. (Except me, of course. I once spent a wedding getting drinks for everyone because I spilled a full English breakfast all over the outfit I was going to wear and ended up going in a white blouse and black skirt. 'Another bottle of dry white? Coming up.')

No matter. The point is: when you're happy high

status, anyone can ask you to do anything and you do it with grace and charm, without losing any of your power. This is very much the person Michelle Obama became towards the end of her husband's presidency. She transformed into the shiniest and most inspiring example of this quality: able to occupy the highest and most prestigious spot in the room while talking to children, charity workers, the homeless, hip-hop stars and the Queen all in exactly the same way. Remember how she got away with touching the Queen very lightly on the back? That, my friends, is happy high status. (The Queen, on the other hand, is high status but she is definitely not happy. This comes across in her public speaking in the way that she seems to endure and tolerate it, not to enjoy it.) What's crucial, though, about Michelle is that – unlike her husband – she was not always this way. She has had to learn how to be happy high status. And if she can do it, we all can.

Status is a state of mind not a position in society

Let's back up. You will probably be thinking, But, Viv, how can I be happy high status if I'm not First Lady of the United States? Surely the happiness and the high status slightly come with the territory. What if I'm a toilet attendant? Or, indeed, a cocktail waitress? How am I supposed to feel happy and high status then?

This is the joy of it. A toilet attendant can be happy

high status. In fact, it's really important for a toilet attendant to be happy high status. Likewise a cocktail waitress.
You may also be thinking, But, Viv, this is supposed to be
an inspiring read about women speakers. Why have you
started with a story about a man? And you will definitely
be thinking, What has this got to do with being a brilliant
public speaker?

Let me explain. Happy high status is the single most
important thing about being a strong public speaker. If
you're genuinely happy high status, it's very hard to have
any interaction that will not be well received by the audience, whether it's one person in an informal meeting or a
crowd of fifty thousand at a massive rally. Happy high status reads up close. And it reads at a vast distance. The
camera picks it up instantly. It's a transmission of energy,
trust and enthusiasm: 'I see you. I don't judge you.' ('You
want a cocktail? Have a cocktail! It doesn't matter that I'm
not your waiter!') But, most importantly, it's an inside job.
It's not about learning how to hold your body, project your
voice, plant your feet or align your spine (although we
should focus on all those things too because they all matter). It's about the most important first principle of how you
present yourself to the world: how you feel inside yourself.
Are you generally comfortable with who you are, conceal-
ing nothing and ready for anything, including being
mistaken for a wait-person? Because that is exactly who
Michelle Obama is. Or, rather, it's who she learned to be.

This quality can't be faked. But it can be acquired, practised and improved upon. Very close to charisma, it's true that some people have it naturally. They are the people we all gravitate towards in social situations because they make us feel comfortable. They tend to have three qualities: they're as interested in us as in themselves; they don't take anything personally; and they have a knack for making everything seem easy and natural. Think about that cocktail interaction again. It's really not that big a deal. And why wouldn't you get a drink at a party for someone? What else are you going to do? Turn around and say, 'Don't you know who I am? Get your own cocktail'? Of course you have to do the right thing, if you're any kind of a good person.

Great speakers are made not born

There is plenty of evidence that Michelle Obama worked hard to get to this level of confidence. And the fact that she worked at it is a good thing because it gives us all hope. Sure, she has the natural attributes of a happy high status person, but she also has the attributes of the people who resist this role: an inbuilt cynicism, a little bit of aloofness, a dose of eye-rolling. (Come on. We've all done it.) She even resisted the status of First Lady for a long time before embracing it and, even then, was not initially happy in the role, taking a while to settle into her own version of it.

It's a well-documented fact that she questioned her husband's choice of political career for some time, and that, of the two of them, she was the more reluctant about either of them seeking high office. Many have remarked that it's this quality that marks her out as the sort of person who would make a great politician: she actually resists power for its own sake and was wary of how it would change her husband. She has said many times that she would never go into politics. And yet she more or less has. It's like the quote from *Twelfth Night*: 'Some are born great, some achieve greatness, and some have greatness thrust upon them.' To be happy high status in the way Michelle Obama has become is to be comfortable with being given greatness, whether you want it or not.

In some ways, this is a fantastic metaphor for what a sudden public-speaking opportunity can feel like when you're not expecting it or didn't ask for it: greatness is being thrust upon you. How you deal with the weight of that greatness is all to do with whether you can cope with being happy and high status at the same time.

It's one thing to accept high status when it means 'at the top of the hierarchy'. Think of political leaders (and queens) who occupy their role with dignity and gravitas. It's quite another to be happy and relaxed about it so that others accept your status but almost don't think about it, let alone feel intimidated by it. This is a real skill. As I've mentioned, not everyone who is high status is happy high status.

And, to be fair, many high-status people manage to be convincing and effective public speakers while leveraging their status and without doing the inner work. Look at Donald Trump. He is high status but he is not happy high status. If you mistake him for a cocktail waiter, you are going to die. And yet he does have a presence as a public speaker: many people find his speeches compelling and many have voted for him on the strength of them. And yet. His speaking does not have true conviction or emotion. It uses rhetorical tricks and catchphrases ('Build a wall!') instead of aiming for connection and empathy. He makes the most of being high status. But think what he could achieve if he were happy high status. (Actually don't think about that. It's never going to happen.)

Happy high status is a state of mind that is not easy to achieve. Not even Michelle Obama just dropped naturally into it. In the early days of Barack Obama's life as a United States senator in 2005, two years before he announced his candidacy for the presidency, Michelle Obama rolled her eyes at a reporter at an event and said, 'Maybe one day he will do something to warrant all this.' That is not a happy high status thing to say. It's a very passive-aggressive thing to say. (Though it's also funny. Kudos.) But as Michelle Obama reduced her job as a hospitals executive to one day a week while her husband pounded the campaign trail, she began to learn how to match up to the status of First Lady and to stop saying things that would undercut her or her husband's status. She learned to be comfortable – happy – with the status. This meant that when she came to speak, she could do so from the heart and not be afraid of being exposed in any way. She would not have to learn to rely on tricks and crowd manipulation. She would be able to say what she wanted to say and people would accept it and listen. (Though not always agree. But that's part of the happy bit of high status: you're happy for other people to sit with their views. You don't have to convince everyone. You're OK with any response, even if it's negative.)

The kind of transformation Michelle Obama effected while in training to be First Lady was all about balancing the two sides of happy high status. The high status bit means no undermining quips that indicate you're not too comfortable in a position of power. It means being comfortable when others expect you to walk in front of them. It means stepping up to take decisions the second they are required. The happy bit means doing it in a stress-free, relaxed way, as if this is the most natural thing in the world to you.

What does this have to do with everyday communication and public speaking? Everything. Because it's about how you show up in the world. It's about signalling to an audience whether you are genuinely happy and relaxed to be there, whether you can take on the mantle of responsibility, whether you can carry them for the duration of what you're about to say.

If this sounds incredibly scary, it doesn't have to be. We all occupy roles in our everyday life in which we are naturally happy high status without thinking about it. We have to be this way with our friends when they're relying on us to drive them somewhere (especially when we are the designated driver and everyone else is drunk). We have to be this way with our children when we're crossing the road with them. We naturally behave in this way when we're buying something in a shop or ordering food in a restaurant. In short, it's the moments in life when we have to take charge in some small, manageable way and we feel completely OK about it. When there's no pressure and no one is really watching, we're totally fine with it. It's when we have to do it on stage that it gets scary.

Perfection is not the aim

The great thing about Michelle Obama as an example of a brilliant public speaker, who had to learn how to be good, is that you can go back and look at all her speeches from the past ten years on YouTube. She delivered the first in 2008, and although it was favourably reviewed at the time (and was credited as one of the reasons Barack Obama got elected), she went on to get so much better. In that first speech she is introduced as 'a loving daughter, wife and mother' to the first bars of 'Signed, Sealed, Delivered'. She hesitates and stumbles over her first two sentences, makes several more errors where she misspeaks and has to repeat herself. In my view she is clearly slowing her speech to calm her nerves. (Which is a great trick, by the way.) She shakes her head too much and uses her hands too frequently. (I'm nit-picking here.) The point is: you can deliver a great speech that is far from perfection.

But the happy high status bit of her is already emerging. She has the characteristic mix of half-jokes and family stories, self-deprecating references to her life with her husband and a hint at the political steel she will channel in later speeches. (Much later. In these early speeches, she was almost exclusively confined to selling herself as a mother and a wife.) She also says a very happy high status thing, about treating people with respect and dignity, 'even if you don't know them – and even if you don't agree with them'. Later in the speech come some forceful arguments (Iraq, healthcare, education) but, interestingly, her heart doesn't seem in it in quite the way it will be in later speeches. She's happy. But she's not 100 per cent high status. Yet. She walks off to a track I cannot imagine she would have chosen herself in a million years: 'Isn't She Lovely?'

That was her first speech of the campaign trail when she was being intensely scrutinized as 'the future first African-American First Lady'. And it wasn't perfect. One review said: 'Michelle Obama lacked the rhetorical ability of her husband and failed to arouse the audience in the way he is capable.' Interestingly, Barack Obama was already twenty months into his campaign when she gave this speech. This is important to remember: she could have spoken earlier in the campaign. She wasn't champing at the bit to give this speech. She wasn't rushing. You can imagine she might have been talked into it a bit. The Michelle Obama we know a decade later, who made headlines with 'When they go low, we go high', was not a born speaker, desperate to get up on the podium. On the other hand, her authenticity was already writ large with that first speech.

I love the YouTube comment that says it all: 'Guys. Can you imagine marrying a girl and later running for office and your wife being able to deliver a speech like this? It's phenomenal.' Maybe not the hardcore feminist response you might be hoping for. But still. Heartfelt. And ultimately vote-winning. This was an early sign of Michelle Obama's strength: wearing high status lightly, authentically, happily.

The importance of looking like you really want to be up there

Once Michelle Obama occupied the role of First Lady and grew into it, her power as a speaker grew exponentially. Crucially, this was not because she was First Lady. Show me any other First Lady's speeches that have been as good as hers. It was not about the office. It was about her relationship to it: she fully owned it. She also had enough grace and generosity to carry the burden: it's not easy to give speeches as First Lady because your critics gripe that you're not elected and why is it any of your business to talk about politics anyway? (Which is a perfectly fair point.) On the other hand, Michelle Obama and the team around her recognized that her ability to step up was inspiring to voters – maybe even more inspiring than seeing politicians do it because, let's face it, they have to: it's their job. When someone gives an amazing speech because they chose to? That really is something.

So when she gave the speech of her life at the 2016 National Democratic Convention in which she talked about her attachment to her daughters, what she hoped for their future and how she marvelled that 'I wake up every morning in a house that was built by slaves', she was ready. It was this moment, I think, that transformed her in people's eyes and revealed her to be a one-woman showcase for happy high status, very different from her early speaking opportunities.

Here she is very still and calm. Her emotions are open, she laughs a lot, she moves her hands but with discipline. She allows natural pauses that show she is controlling the speech: it is not controlling her. (Eight years earlier, it did feel as if she just wanted to get through it. In 2016, she's enjoying it.) She allows herself to speak faster because she's comfortable. The message is clear: 'I'm doing this the way I want to. Get on board.' Unsurprisingly, by the time she and her husband left the White House a few months later, her public-speaking fee was estimated at $200,000 for one speech. (Half that of her husband but, come on, he was POTUS.) I think that sum is an extremely conservative estimate. I would save this money up myself in coins, some-how, just to meet her and make some coffee for her. I wouldn't expect her to speak. She can just sit there being happy high status and I'll look at her. (The coffee would be a special chicory blend and I would serve it in cups that I had made myself in a pottery class.)

I realize I'm now sounding like an idealist or, at very least, a yoga devotee trapped in downward dog. (Happy high status is actually a very Buddhist kind of idea. Buddha regarded social rankings as worthless in terms of the quest for personal happiness. In fact, he recognized that an obsession with social ranking often brought people great misery.) It's easy to dismiss happy high status as an idea because it sounds fine for anyone born with this quality. What about the rest of us? When I first found out about happy high status, I felt angry. Of course it's easy for George Clooney to bring the cocktail. He has nothing to lose. He has loads of money, he's extremely handsome, and every-one loves him. Bringing the cocktail will be an amusing story for him to tell his friends. But what about someone who is less fortunate in life? Why should they lower them-selves to bring the cocktail? Why should they have a smile on their face while they clean the toilet for you?

It's exactly this attitude that you have to examine in yourself if you're going to approach an audience (whether a crowd of one or – as Michelle Obama faced on that first outing in 2008 – four thousand). If your attitude is one of meanness and self-protection ('Why should I bring the cocktail? I'm not a waiter'), the audience will feel it. If your attitude is one of relaxed generosity and openness ('Sure, I can get you a cocktail!'), they'll feel that too. The more you think about happy high status, the more you learn to observe when you're embodying it. And the more you recognize the times when you're not. Only a superhuman could be happy high status all the time. It takes practice. But it really is the first step to being relaxed as a speaker: before you've even said anything, you've stepped out with that intention and it reads extraordinarily clearly.

In my experience, some women don't so much need help with public speaking as with the self-doubt and self-loathing that hold them back from getting involved in it. And I think a lot of that has to do with discomfort at being happy high status. It's important to say 'some women'. There's a younger generation on YouTube, podcasts and vlogs, who have no problems making their voices heard, whose voices scream 'happy' and who have no problem occupying the maximum amount of status – although I hear doubt and hesitancy from them when it comes to being featured on the hallowed 'proper' platforms of old media. Like the podcaster with millions of downloads who wanted to turn down a request for BBC *Woman's Hour* because she was afraid she'd be shown up as not worthy. Amusingly, I've heard women from established media outlets turning down podcasts for the opposite reason: they're worried they won't sound hip or relaxed enough or that the freewheeling nature of things will expose them.

This is the stuff we need to fight back against: the fear of getting it wrong, getting caught out, being seen as 'not good enough'. Ironically it's the ability to get it wrong, be out of your depth, take a risk and maybe even fail spectacularly that qualifies you as happy high status. When you are truly happy and truly high status, you're not afraid of losing your status on such a small thing – or, indeed, on anything. You have the confidence that you will hold your status, even if it threatens to be undermined. Do you see Barack Obama turning down Zach Galifianakis who wants to talk to him and ideally make him look stupid (because that will go viral) while he sits next to a pot plant? (This was for the comedy show *Between Two Ferns*, where a politician is 'interviewed' by Galifianakis, who asks nonsensical questions.) No, you do not. (We have yet, however, to see Donald Trump appear in such a context, for all his much-vaunted very bigly high status.) Do you see Michelle Obama turning down the opportunity to dance hip-hop in front of a real-life crowd of thousands and a television crowd of millions while knocking on her fiftieth birthday? No, you do not. These are people who are so comfortable in their status that they're not afraid to risk losing it. They understand that status is not something that is given by others, as in 'We'll make you President.' It is something that you can only take for yourself: 'I am your President.'

Of course no one's perfect when it comes to this stuff, not even Michelle Obama. No one can maintain constant happy high status. We all get tired. We all lose our temper. We all have bad days. Michelle Obama dropped her status, for example, when Melania Trump came lumbering towards her with an unanticipated Tiffany's box at Donald Trump's inauguration. The exasperation on Michelle's face was clear: this was a breach of protocol and she was momentarily stumped as to how to handle it. Barack Obama – long-term at ease with happy high status because, let's face it, he was born to it – raced to the rescue, grabbed the package and took it inside the building. This was his own George Clooney cocktail moment. Given the chance to practise high status more often, we'd all have dealt with that ridiculous package as elegantly as he did.

The best thing about happy high status is when it becomes so practised and natural that you embody it without thinking. It's sheer practice that means rock stars, TV presenters, models and actors are able to transmit it effortlessly. (Did I mention that it also helps if you're very attractive? Although being happy high status will make you seem more attractive to people anyway.)

Barack Obama was embodying it so fully and so unconsciously that he once caught a fly effortlessly while discussing regulatory reform on live television. The *New York Times*' report of this extraordinary example of happy high status behaviour recalled the words of Mr Miyagi in *Karate Kid*: 'Man who catch fly with chopstick accomplish anything.' (A headline quote that's acceptable because it's from *Karate Kid*, OK?) In fact, what Obama did was very simple: he allowed himself to drop into the zone where he was in control of everything in the most relaxed and easy-going way. Given a few extra seconds, he would probably have served the fly a cocktail.

Time, though, to turn the statement around and rewrite the words of Mr Miyagi. A woman who can harness happy high status can accomplish anything. No chopsticks needed.

Tips and Tricks

— Happy high status is a state of mind as well as ease in your body. A lot of the time when people present, saying, 'I'm afraid of public speaking,' what they really mean is 'I'm afraid to take status.'

— Michelle Obama's upper arms are no coincidence. Lots of voice coaches will say that good speaking starts with looking after your body. Having a strong core, healthy lungs and good posture will support your voice – and also make the audience more at ease with you. (If you look unhealthy, the audience will be distracted, wondering whether you feel OK or whether something's the matter. If you really are unwell but having to make a speech anyway, the happy high status thing to do is to acknowledge it with a joke at the beginning: 'Don't come too close, by the way. I have a cold.' Then ignore it and get on with what you're doing. If you're so unwell that you're making the audience uncomfortable, you probably shouldn't be there.)

— In every situation you're in, think: What would someone who is happy high status be doing now? Happy high status people are in control but generous and easy-going. They are not rude or short-tempered.

— There are no hard and fast rules to this, and status is often very individual. It can be very powerful to be the first person in the room to speak, then say nothing afterwards, making sure you're sitting upright with your core engaged while looking relaxed and ready for everything. That is usually the most happy high status posture in a meeting.

— Before a speech, think about the happy high status way to approach what you're going to say. This is a fine balance. You need to avoid being self-deprecating (this is to deny your status) while finding ways to engage the audience, whether that's with stories or anecdotes or by varying the tone of your voice.

— Think about happy high status posture and physicality: openness, strong spine, relaxed gestures, stillness of the head, your weight evenly planted through your feet.

Exercises

— At the next meeting you're at with more than four or five people, take a look around the room and notice who is high status, who is low status, whose status is ambiguous. Watch and see if it changes over the course of the meeting. Observe others and ask yourself, 'Who is being happy high status here? Who is high status but unhappy? Who is happy but not taking any status?' At the next meeting, think about the status you project and how you could behave differently to change it.

— Use this meditation/visualization exercise to lift your mood in an emergency or just ahead of speaking. Find a quiet, private space where you can be alone. Stand in a relaxed, confident posture with feet planted hip-width apart, shoulders back, chest out. Close your eyes. Take deep breaths. Imagine a time when you felt happy high status. A time when you felt proud, confident, ready to take on the world. With every breath in, deepen this feeling and relax into it. Let yourself really feel it for three or four minutes. Now open your eyes and allow yourself to carry as much of that feeling as possible with you.

— Write down three times when you felt happy high status. These moments in life will not be the same for everyone but here are some ideas: 'The time I won a race when I was at school'; 'When I passed my driving test after seven attempts'; 'The moment I held my baby in my arms for the first time.' It ideally needs to be a moment that gave you a feeling of awe, exhilaration or achievement. Write these on a card and keep it with you. If you're feeling droopy, look at the card and remember how you felt in those moments. Those feelings haven't gone anywhere and you can drop down into them at any time.

3

Be More Amy: Power Poses, Internal Strength and How to Project Presence

Speaking doesn't have to be showy and flashy

While being happy high status is a way to pull people in easily and make them feel all warm and fuzzy around you, the add-on is that elusive thing called 'presence'. Presence is slightly different from 'status' or 'happy high status'. While status confers the external message that you are ready to lead and other people should pay attention to you, presence is the projection of how you are feeling right here, right now. It is slightly calmer and less showy than being happy high status. Presence draws other people towards you because you seem open, engaged and fully, well, present. You can experience it in yourself: you are alive to the moment; you are not distracted by anything (including your own insecurity); you are calm and focused. While happy high status is a state or an attitude, projecting presence is an action. Even if you are not feeling happy high status, you can still relax enough to be fully present.

The following are not presence: checking your phone just before you go on stage; getting distracted during your speech because you're annoyed with yourself about something you did wrong (which, probably, no one else noticed);

failing to address a major distraction in the room (like a window smashing) because it's not in your script. If you are truly focused, you can incorporate all of these things and not be bothered by them.

The phenomenon of presence is explored at length in the most-watched TED Talk of all time (at the time of writing), by body-language expert Amy Cuddy. She argues that one of the markers of presence is confidence and that it's possible to achieve presence by focusing on how you hold your body before you start to speak. She calls this the 'power pose'. There's an imperceptible exchange that goes on between mind and body, explains Cuddy. You can fool your mind into thinking you're more confident than you really are by taking a power pose for two minutes or more. (Stand, like Wonderwoman, with hands on hips or with your hands held aloft, like Usain Bolt crossing the finishing line.) She advises taking yourself to one side before a nerve-racking event, like a job interview or a speaking opportunity, and taking the pose for a few minutes. It looks idiotic and makes you feel stupid (I advise doing it in a toilet cubicle, if you can find one large enough) but – from personal experience – it does work. I can't say it's any better than sitting and doing breathing exercises for two minutes, but there's something in it.

Don't be confused by some of the hype around power poses that has swept the corporate world since Cuddy's TED Talk first came out. They are not poses to use in public or while you're speaking, although there are some hilarious pictures of politicians seemingly misunderstanding the technique and standing like Superman at press conferences. Cuddy's tips fall under the same heading as 'speaker preparation' or 'meditation' or 'mindfulness training'. They're like doing a yoga pose before an interview to relax. They are to be used to boost your internal feelings about yourself, not to project power to others. According to Cuddy's research, subjects' testosterone levels went up and cortisol levels, connected to stress, fell.

There has been some debate about the science behind Cuddy's findings and I can see that these studies can't be easy to replicate on a mass scale. But let's give her the benefit of the doubt. Because Cuddy touches on something really interesting here: the contrast between how you present externally (what other people see) and how you think of yourself internally (how you feel). Ideally you want both of these things in balance. Absolutely ideally, you want not to have to think about them at all, of course. In reality, there may be times when the two are not in sync because you're tired or nervous. The first thing that will give you away is your body language. We tend to hunch our shoulders or make ourselves smaller when we're feeling anxious.

Power poses are not about other people (because you do the poses privately to affect your mental state). They're about fooling yourself into believing that you can channel

Wonderwoman or Usain Bolt. There are two sides to presence. One is internal: if you adopt the right posture (before or during an event), it will strengthen your power, poise and confidence – and your body will fool your mind into thinking you're getting away with it. (This is the physical version of 'fake it till you make it'.) The other is external: the right presence signalled through posture and stance is a message to others about who is in charge.

Your imperfect presence is enough

Cuddy's theories are about giving ourselves a boost without expecting to transform into Wonderwoman or Usain Bolt. This is about tricking your brain into feeling confident, so that you can relax and be present. It's not about trying to present yourself as an actual superhero. Cuddy gives a reminder of this in her opener to her TED Talk, 'Your Body Language May Shape Who You Are'. What's even more interesting is how she delivers the talk. She doesn't worry too much about illustrating her own examples. Her posture is not perfect: she is a little hunched and doesn't come across as poised. She uses her hands a lot, verging on too much. Although she's not unconfident, she does not radiate self-assurance or exuberance: she is calm, discreet, academic. Her nerves are evident: she says 'um' five times in the first sixty seconds of her talk.

Nonetheless her talk is phenomenally successful (47

million views at the last count and transcribed into fifty-one languages). So, there is clearly nothing wrong with it. People love it. You don't have to be perfect, we learn. You just have to be a plausible, comfortable version of yourself, even if that isn't perfectly poised. How does she get away with being a speaker who is not happy high status? Presence. She is comfortable in her own skin and she draws us in. She has a pleasant, conversational tone. She shows a degree of vulnerability. She is definitely not perfect.

You can see the same in TED Talks by Elizabeth Gilbert ('Your Elusive Creative Genius'), Brené Brown ('The Power of Vulnerability') and Susan Cain ('The Power of Introverts'). These speakers are not trying to blow you away, although they all have moments of levity and humour, which are designed to raise the mood of the room. They don't project the intensity or direct leadership of a Michelle Obama speech, but they are just as commanding in their own way.

Elizabeth Gilbert opens her speech with almost as many 'ums' as Amy Cuddy. She seems cautious and a little uncertain. But this is not because she's nervous (or it seems not): it's because her talk is going to be intimate and vulnerable and she's preparing the audience for that. She wanders around the stage, overuses her hands and takes a while to settle in. Again – it doesn't matter. It's good. It's compelling and it's real because she has presence.

Brené Brown, the academic researcher who talks and writes brilliantly on bravery, shame and vulnerability, is more relaxed and clearly an experienced speaker (and has the brashness of her native Texas, which she often references in her talks). But she too 'allows' herself to make mistakes, to say 'um', to let some of her anecdotes look spontaneous and under-rehearsed.

It's OK to be understated

These are all great examples of how you don't need to be some kind of blow-them-away powerhouse to own the room. You can be geeky, quiet and even a bit closed off. Perhaps the most interesting example of this is Susan Cain. Her subject matter is introversion and she says from the beginning that she herself is introverted. She is the opposite of a high-energy motivational speaker. Sure, she could lead – in her own way – but she is not a happy high status kind of person. Her power comes from understatement, self-belief and, yes, presence.

In her TED Talk, Cain holds herself with impressive stillness, she never moves too far from the spot where she begins and she uses her arms with discipline. She controls her natural introversion by taking her speech one thought at a time and pausing between ideas. Her posture and the way she speaks embody the message behind her talk: you don't have to pretend to be someone you're not; you don't have to 'pass' as an extrovert. You can be who you are. But you need to be fully present.

What do I mean by this in the context of speaking? What does presence look and feel like? Most of all presence is about looking and feeling comfortable in a space. It suggests readiness. This is not quite the same as happy high status, which suggests availability to lead or to command. (Hence the status.) Presence is more neutral and open to anything. If you look at how Susan Cain stands in the space during her TED Talk, it's very impressive, yet low-key. She is on a huge stage. There is a vast audience in front of her reaching round horizontally on both sides of her. (Instead of reaching far up or far back.) She could be tempted to be lost on that stage and shrink into herself. Or she could attempt to reach everyone on either side by turning constantly. Instead she stands her ground and lets the audience come to her. She uses the space a little; she is not rooted to the spot. But she absorbs the moment and does what she came there to do. It's very powerful because she looks as if she's treating it like it's not a big deal. And this is exactly what we should all be aiming for.

Yet she is clearly not a person who is comfortable in the spotlight. She says so herself. She is an introvert. She doesn't like talking to large groups of people. She argues that our whole society is biased towards extroverts and I think the same is true for our (false) perception of public speaking: we think you need to be confident, in-your-face and loud. You don't. You just need to say what you came to say, without getting caught up in doubt and fear.

The same goes for leadership, says Cain: introverts are passed over in favour of extroverts when studies show that introverts are good leaders because they are good at giving power and agency to others. She mentions Eleanor Roosevelt, Rosa Parks and Gandhi as examples of introverts who had to show leadership and take the spotlight 'even though every bone in their bodies was telling them not to'. I wonder how many of us – no matter whether we define ourselves as introverted or extroverted – count ourselves out of opportunities to lead or to speak because we feel we can't fit some stereotypical mould.

All of these women's talks show that audiences are not interested in the stereotype. They just want to hear and see something interesting and heartfelt from a speaker with presence.

To 'own the room' does not mean that you need to blow everyone away with your charisma and greatness. It means that, instead of being overwhelmed by the speech and trying to mould yourself into something you're not, you find ways of being yourself and making the speech fit around you, even if you're a quiet, modest person.

I've worked with women who have had to give extremely high-pressure, career-changing speeches in front of hundreds of colleagues in male-dominated environments. Early on in their preparation such women sometimes freeze. They worry that there is no precedent for a woman speaking in that space, or become anxious about 'representing' women. I always encourage them to look inwards and find a way to bring something of themselves to a speech, instead of thinking too much about what has come before: 'What are you going to do in this one twenty-minute speech? Try to erase thousands of years of patriarchy? That's quite a lot of pressure you're putting on yourself. Is that the best use of your time? Wouldn't you be better off just turning up and giving the best account of yourself and your knowledge that you can, whatever that looks like?'

'Be with us how you are'

One of the most important things I learned during a temporary addiction to attending clowning workshops (which I wouldn't wish on my worst enemy because they're extremely stressful and unfunny, though very useful for developing performance skills) came from the master clown Philip Burgers: 'Be with us how you are.' What he meant by this was: 'Don't pretend to be something you're not. Don't be fake. If you're excited that the audience is applauding you, show your excitement. If you're disappointed that someone is leaving the room, show it.'

We are trained from an early age to fake politeness, charisma, enthusiasm, interest and passion in our day-to-day life and in front of groups of people. Clown training says forget all that: be who you really are, right now in this

HOW TO OWN THE ROOM

moment. That isn't always possible in a work context where you have to fake enthusiasm for, say, a marketing presentation. But if you can bring a flavour of that authentic presence, your audience will appreciate it. If you say, 'I really didn't want to give this presentation today as I have a stinking cold', it's not a terrible way to start, provided you don't moan the entire way through. Honesty is not a free pass to complain that you don't want to give the speech. If you really don't want to give it, don't.

Cuddy's power poses are good for raising your internal confidence level. That in itself helps with presence. Perhaps even more useful is the idea of honesty and being alive to the possibility of mistakes, nerves, rejection and failure. Great speaking – even good speaking – is not about avoiding making mistakes and never failing. It's about being open to the moment, being present. It's about being ready to throw out what you were going to say, because you've just realized that the person speaking before you covered that ground or the mood of the room has changed. Or because you can barely speak for flu symptoms and you're going to have to acknowledge that fact to the audience. It's about not fearing that they will reject you because you just admitted that you feel uncomfortable at being there. Those are good risks to take.

Presence is also a good cheat if you struggle with being happy high status. The difficulty with happy high status is that it usually requires a certain amount of charisma. If that doesn't sit well with you, it's not worth faking it. Instead take as much status as you feel comfortable with and aim for presence instead. You can see this very clearly in the TED Talks of Brené Brown, Amy Cuddy and Elizabeth Gilbert. They are all close to happy high status but they don't quite project the intensity and dynamism of Michelle Obama. I mean this as an observation, not as a criticism. The point is: all speakers are different. The trick is to find your own style.

This is another moment where honesty is a helpful device. Susan Cain uses it. She admits in her speech that she doesn't like public speaking and had to force herself to become good at it. I would hit you and/or possibly bury you alive if you ever uttered the phrase 'Unaccustomed as I am to public speaking', but if you add a genuine disclaimer, like 'I felt uncomfortable at the prospect of speaking to you today . . .' if you really mean it and open up by explaining why, that is admirable and useful.

The first rule of presence: open up and stand tall

If I'm working on presentation skills with a group, one of the first things I will do is an acting exercise that demonstrates the effect of status on state of mind easily and effectively. I ask people to close their eyes and imagine they're feeling nervous, anxious and cowed. Sometimes I'll ask them to remember a time in their life when they felt like that. (If I'm feeling really mean. Taking yourself back to a memory can be more painful and real than trying to conjure a feeling artificially. But it's often more useful.) I ask them to hold that feeling or memory in mind, then walk around the room and introduce themselves. Without having to think about it, they will avoid eye contact, adopt a shrunken posture and generally project embarrassment and shame. Ah, who doesn't know it well? I ask them to stop, close their eyes and remember a moment when they felt proud of themselves, to imagine themselves in that moment. Immediately their heads pull up (like a puppet on a string with the thread going right through the top of the head), their shoulders pull back and their chests puff out. They make strong eye contact and smile. They project self-assurance, confidence, love, joy. (I know, I know. I get a bit carried away and emotional with all this stuff. But it's true, they do.)

This is so obvious, yet we don't think about it when we're preparing to present or to speak. We think instead about our state of mind. We concentrate on our anxiety, on the details of what we're about to present (Can we remember all the statistics? What was that quote again?), on the person in the room we're most afraid of, on the teacher at school who told us we were rubbish at public speaking. We think of so many things that are irrelevant and unhelpful – and often untrue.

It would be so much more helpful if we concentrated

on (a) adopting (or faking) a positive state of mind (focusing on a time when we felt proud, truly visualizing it and allowing ourselves to feel the emotions of that moment in our bodies) and (b) adopting (or faking) the posture that goes with it. The two (state of mind + posture) then interact to produce the illusion of presence. And the illusion of presence can very quickly switch into its reality. If you stand as though you have presence, your mind will start to think, Hey, maybe I do have presence. And if your mind is thinking, I'm remembering the time I did something truly great, your body will be unable to shrink into a Quasimodo shape. (No offence to Quasimodo. He, too, had a voice in his own way and struggled to be heard. Power poses might have helped.)

If you are thinking, But, Viv, I have never done anything truly great so I cannot adopt the posture of greatness, then you're just not trying hard enough. The truly great moment of pride that will help you access presence probably won't have been winning the Nobel Prize for peace or opening a centre for orphans in the name of Mother Teresa. You can remember the time you birthed a baby (always a good one in my view, provided this was a positive experience for you), the time you were praised for a piece of work or the time you baked a really fabulous cake. Pride about small things is good: it is practice for feeling pride about the big things. Pride is pride. It doesn't matter if it comes from the perfect lemon drizzle loaf or from Olympic gold.

How come some annoying people have natural presence without having to think about it?

It's true that just as some people have natural charisma or radiate happy high status, others naturally have presence. We could split hairs for a long time arguing whether there is a difference between the two qualities. I think they differ slightly. A yoga teacher might have presence but little need for charisma. A politician can be happy high status without having much presence. And a comedian might have a lot of charisma but it could be part of their act that they project not being truly present and/or are comfortably low status. (This is what Woody Allen does, for example.) These qualities differ between individuals and often we cannot agree on them. Some people warm to certain performers and say they almost have an 'aura'. Looking at the same person, others may feel completely differently. There's something mysterious about the qualities that make us trust other people and warm to them.

What matters for you as an individual is what is useful for you. If you feel you have natural charisma but you struggle to focus and be in the moment, then you need to focus on your presence. Similarly, if you have status and take up space very easily, perhaps because you've been in a senior role for a long time and are used to being listened to, you may want to think about bringing a bit more charisma and spontaneity to what you do by being more informal or referring to some of your vulnerabilities.

Of course, some people have these qualities naturally and don't have to think about it. And they are the people we want to emulate and channel. Look out for people whose company seems easy, comfortable, relaxed. What is it about the way they interact with others that makes them feel this way? Just observing it in others is hugely useful. These things are often highly subjective and individualized. Some people will achieve this effect by making strong eye contact. Others will achieve it by gently making sure they include everyone in a group. We all need to figure out our own idea of presence.

Tips and Tricks

— If you want to project presence, you need to focus on how you feel internally. Meditation apps are good for this. (I recommend Headspace and Buddhify.) They have calmed me at times when my mind is racing and I know I'm not going to be able to connect with an audience. They take you out of all your whirling thoughts and reconnect you to the present moment.

— Voicing your thoughts in a speech can be a bold and empowering move but it takes guts. The more you do it, the more present you will seem. But there is nothing wrong with a speaker who steps out of what they prepared for a second and says calmly, 'I just want to take a moment to say how much it means to me to have your attention.' Or: 'I just want to say how glad I am to be here.' Or even, simply: 'Thanks so much for coming today.' (You have to mean it.) Really say these things: don't mumble them and throw them away. If you feel bold enough, connect with someone in the audience when you say it.

Exercises

— Repeat the exercise on feeling grounded (chapter 1, page 23). Shoulders back. Chest forward. Feet hip width apart. Feel the ground with the soles of your feet. (You can also do this in high heels. I used to worry a lot about whether I was doing it properly in them. It's fine.) If you have some time before you start, think about breathing through the soles of your feet as you breathe in and out. Draw the breath up from the ground. Now think about how present you feel. Try to fix that feeling in your mind so that it becomes familiar. This is the state of mind you're aiming to speak from.

— Think about something you would like to share in a speech that is special to you or makes you feel vulnerable. Do you have an insecurity that you have improved upon? What is the problem you have overcome? What's the life challenge that other people struggle with that you have also struggled with? Make a list of ten ideas. Keep them to yourself for now. You can bring them out later. These are all things you could talk about in a TEDx Talk. Or they are things you could incorporate into an inspirational talk at work. You don't need to tell your whole life story. You can tell one short personal story, even in three sentences, then open it up to something more general. Watch how Susan Cain does this in her

TED Talk. First she talks about how it was for her when she turned up at summer camp as a shy child with a suitcase of books. She moves swiftly into discussing statistics and research about how we treat shy people in society. Good speakers move easily and quickly between the personal and the universal.

— Choose one of your ten ideas and resolve that you will use it in a speech within the next three months. By the time you've finished this book, you may be ready to apply for a TEDx Talk (see p. 228). Or perhaps you can find another occasion to discuss your idea. If it has a direct link to your work experience, is there a colleague you can talk to about how you could grow it into a speaking opportunity?

4

Be More Virginia: Shakespeare's Sister, the Angel in the House and a Pace of One's Own

The more complex your ideas, the slower your speech

When thinking about how fast to talk, the ultimate bench-mark for speaking at your own pace is Virginia Woolf. She spoke slowly. Languidly, even. It's not really possible to say much more about her speaking style as we have only eight minutes of audio to go on. Sadly, with only one known recording of her voice and obviously no video, we can only guess at her impact as a speaker and only speculate as to whether this was a typical example of her speaking. What I'm saying is this: I'm reading quite a lot into this one record-ing. It was made for BBC radio in 1937 and features her reading an essay called 'Craftsmanship', which was pub-lished as part of the collection *The Death of a Moth and Other Essays*.

It gives us at least a flavour of how she must have sounded to the audiences who attended her public lec-tures. She speaks in a slow, deliberate, clipped way. Her pace is almost like that of someone reading poetry over a metronome. I like to think that in real life, when she was not reading an essay into a microphone, she would have spoken even more slowly and deliberately. It's almost hypnotic and very old-fashioned. Think of Dame Maggie Smith reading from the Bible in the driest tones imaginable and you're part of the way there.

In her day Virginia Woolf was not known as a prolific speaker but she did give lectures. It is a little-remembered fact that before *A Room of One's Own* was published as a book in 1929, it first appeared as a series of two lectures, written to be read aloud at the women-only colleges, Girton and Newnham, at the University of Cambridge in 1928. This was where Woolf worked out the ideas that were eventually to appear in print. It was here that she rehearsed the book's argument that if a woman is to succeed as a fiction writer she 'must have money and a room of her own'.

She went on to imagine the life of a fictional Judith Shakespeare – 'Shakespeare's sister' – and her chances if she had wanted to follow the same path as her brother. Perhaps not surprisingly, Woolf judged that she 'would have been so thwarted and hindered by other people, so tortured and pulled asunder by her own contrary instincts, that she must have lost her health and sanity to a certainty'. If we're thinking about pace, these are not ideas you're going to gallop through. You'll linger on them. I can imagine Woolf giving the audience the beady eye as she went along.

Later on, in 1931, Woolf gave a speech to a women's group entitled 'Professions for Women', which was to be a sequel to *A Room of One's Own*. It was later published in *The Death of the Moth and Other Essays*. In that speech she talked about a part of herself that she had had to cut off in order to survive: it was the self-deprecating, self-sacrificing, self-denying part. She talked about encountering a 'phantom' (a projection of herself), whom she came to think of as 'The Angel in the House'. These are complex ideas both spoken aloud and on the page and it's easy to see that they are well suited to a strictly restrained pace where the audience has time to take them in.

'The Angel in the House' was the part of herself that told her she was selfish and wrong to want to be a writer and to express her opinion. The Angel in the House is a martyr who devotes herself to her household and has no wants or needs of her own. 'If there was a chicken, she took the leg. If there was a draught she sat in it.' The Angel in the House is not only self-sacrificing: she actively seeks out misery and makes life difficult for herself. (Come on, she doesn't need to sit in the draught.) This phantom began to bias Woolf's work to the extent that it paralysed her. 'The shadow of her wings fell on my page; I heard the rustling of her skirts in the room.' And so, in her imagination, Woolf does what she must do and kills her. 'Had I not killed her, she would have killed me.' This is powerful stuff from a woman who is sick of eating chicken legs.

We also need to kill the Angel when we're speaking. This is Virginia Woolf's way of talking about 'the inner critic', the voice inside all of us that says: 'You're not good enough'; 'You shouldn't be doing this anyway'; 'This work isn't for you'; 'Who are you to stand up and say something?' The Angel will prevent you from speaking your mind and saying what you need to say. She will make you second-guess yourself and worry that someone else could say a lot better what you have to say. She will make you think that you had better hurry up when you're talking so that someone more important can have their turn.

It's not easy to do this, even Virginia Woolf will tell you. Telling the truth about your own experiences as a woman, she said, was extraordinarily difficult. It is all very well to fight for a room of one's own and an income of five hundred pounds a year to provide you with the time to write, but questions remain about the room. As Woolf asks: 'How are you going to furnish it? How are you going to decorate it? Who are you going to share it with and upon what terms?' These are the questions all of us must answer. Clearly, Woolf's unspoken advice is that we have to fight the Angel. And the other unspoken advice is: speak as slowly and deliberately as I do, if you want your complex and nuanced ideas to be understood.

Pace is an individual thing

As a general point, most people need to slow down when they're speaking publicly. It is, though, an extremely personal thing. It's about context. We don't all need to dress up like someone out of the Bloomsbury set and speak as slowly and carefully as if we're in a production of *My Fair Lady*. However, people become obsessed by speed.

In speaking workshops in offices, it's one of the things I'm asked about most often. And when people get me into a work environment to 'fix' someone's speaking, I'm often told that it's because 'they speak too fast'. This isn't an unfair criticism, as anyone who has been to a work event where people are speaking will realize. Loads of people do speak too fast, particularly poor speakers. It's hard to find anyone who speaks too slowly.

As a rule, going more slowly than you think you need to is a good idea. Voice coach Caroline Goyder puts it simply and memorably: 'Those who pause naturally, 3.5 times per minute, are the most successful at influencing their audience.'

Three point five times per minute ... Blimey. That sounds excruciating. And in everyday conversation, it is. But when you're speaking in front of people it's not an everyday conversation. And you've got to give them a chance to register what you're saying. For most people, until they've practised and got used to it, that is going to feel like an uncomfortable amount of pausing. But it really isn't. And it's more important to think about how something comes across to an audience (who will be grateful for the thinking time when you pause) rather than how it sounds to you (which is as if you're talking painfully slowly).

It's always a good idea to focus more on the people in your audience than it is to focus on yourself. Are you speaking slowly enough for your points to land? Could there be anyone in the room who is slightly hard of hearing? What about if they're not a native speaker of the language you're using? Or if they're not completely up to speed on the topic you're addressing? What if someone in the room is simply a bit hung-over and wishing they were at home in bed? Let's face it, in every room at least one person falls into that final category. It always helps me to think of the hung-over person when I start. First, at least I'm not them. (Hopefully not, especially if I'm speaking.) Second, I want them to understand, not feel left out and not wish they'd stayed at home.

The thing about speed, though, is that it's subjective. When I've been called in to do something about speed-talkers in a company, the 'problem' speaker may present as someone who 'talks too fast' but her issue often turns out to be something completely different. I've worked with adept, confident and charismatic speakers whose natural speed is fast. If they slow down too much, they lose their edge. If your strengths include fluency, energy and a fast mind, they will get lost if you over-coach yourself into slowing down. You'd be much better advised to harness your natural energy during the most dynamic parts of your speech, and slow down during the bits that are more complicated or where you're making important points that need to be remembered. This is why it's so important to get to know yourself as a speaker and find out how you come across to others. If your strength is to dazzle people with your brilliance, you may need to be able to speak fast. But not so fast that everyone is blinded by science.

The trick is to watch your audience and listen to them: are they following you at that speed? If they are, you can stay fast. It's crazy to imagine that an audience can't keep up in the right circumstances. Comedians like Joan Rivers, Michael McIntyre and Lee Mack did not make their careers by pausing naturally 3.5 times a minute. They developed a style in which they could harness their natural dynamism and restlessness, then channel it into a way of communicating with which others could keep up without getting exhausted.

Again, though, this is subjective and contextual. These people did not make their careers on the motivational-speaker circuit. Not everyone enjoys mile-a-minute comedy. The tricks and hallmarks of those performances are not necessarily useful in a work context. Even at TED, the gold standard for great speaking in recent times, anything approaching the rhythm or patter of stand-up comedy is frowned upon. That is the difference between an information download (what you're required to give in a work context) and entertainment (or art, if you insist on calling stand-up comedy 'art' and let's assume that I do).

Context is everything

When judging speed and how much you can adapt an opportunity to your natural style (or whether you need to conform to a different standard), this is also the difference between a ticketed performance and a work event. At a ticketed performance, people have chosen to buy into it and have probably done some research into what's going on and why they might like it. At a work event no one has expressly chosen to be there. In that situation, you have a similar duty to a stand-up comedian – to please your audience – and you can use some of the same tricks (be generous, talk in a way that's appropriate for the circumstances, be surprising but in a good way). But there are some tricks from stand-up comedy that you probably can't use – swearing for effect, doing annoying comedy-style crowd work, and referring to your audience in a cheesy way as 'ladies and gentlemen'. This depends on your industry but the more corporate the context, the less likely these devices are to be appropriate.

I mention all this because there's a trend, since the advent of TED, vlogging and the rise of live events, for people to act as if they have to be as good as a performer on *Live at the Apollo*. I don't mean that speakers expect to make the audience laugh in the way a comedian would, but that their 'performance' should be just as slick and professional – TV-ready, if you like. This is completely unrealistic. If you see someone on *Live at the Apollo*, they will have been recorded doing their best twenty minutes, which they might have worked on for five years. Of those twenty minutes, five will be used. Their performance also represents thousands of hours of exposure to crowds and of getting their ego used to being on stage and under lights. It's insane to expect to replicate that with a month's PowerPoint rehearsal.

One of the first tricks to becoming a better speaker is to lower your expectations of yourself, dial down your ego and be honest and realistic about the impact and reach of what you're doing. If you're talking to twenty people at a work presentation, don't treat it as if you've been asked to give the Gettysburg Address. I'm pretty sure Virginia Woolf would have understood this. She used a particular pace and tone because she was recording for the BBC. I imagine the ladies of Cambridge University would have appreciated a similarly leisurely vocal stroll. Holding forth down the pub, she probably gabbled away like the rest of us.

Investigate objectively what works for you

Why do we find the 'slow down' advice so hard to take? And why does our own pace sound so different from others'? I frequently work with people who can't hear how quickly they're speaking. We often have no idea how fast we sound to others. One of the best things you can do for yourself as a speaker (although not as a human being: it can be excruciating) is to record yourself and play it back so that you can listen to the pace of your speech. Ideally listen to it with someone else for objective feedback.

Usually when we listen back to ourselves we focus not on how fast we're speaking but on how weird we sound or how badly we worded something or how we keep saying 'um' and 'er'. The last is a particular problem of mine, which I've been trying to iron out for years. It has nothing to do with being hesitant or not confident: it's just a speech tic that I struggle to, er, eliminate. As you can tell from a number of the top twenty-five TED Talkers (who regularly 'um' and 'er'), it's not that big an issue, but it's good to eliminate these 'fillers': it helps you control the pace of your speech if you're focused on not saying 'um' and 'er'. Slowing down can help your sense and fluidity: just pause and breathe instead of saying 'er' at the start of a sentence.

This may be controversial but I believe that a speech can never be delivered too slowly. Obviously that's not true of stand-up comedy. But for an information download (as many work communications are) or a celebratory speech (at a wedding) or a business negotiation with a lot of detail, you won't regret speaking slowly, even if you feel you're speaking uncomfortably clearly. This is a great thing to demonstrate in front of a group. In a workshop I will secretly brief someone to speak so slowly that they feel as if they want to die of boredom. I will then ask the rest of the group for feedback. 'It was lovely and clear,' they say.

Of course, one of the reasons people have such problems with the pacing of their speech is that they're nervous and they want to get it over with. 'What's really boring for an audience is when a speaker gallops through their content because they don't want to waste the audience's time,' says Caroline Goyder. Assume your audience wants to hear from you so you don't need to rush. There are lots of interesting contradictions around public speaking and performing, which only become evident once you give yourself a chance to have a go at them.

I know many women who are shy in everyday life, hate small-talk at parties and are not fans of speaking in a group, yet eventually discover they are brilliant at public speaking. Similarly, just because someone is the life and soul of the party and very comfortable speaking in group situations, it doesn't mean she'll find it easy to speak into a microphone at a big public event. These are very different disciplines that require different states of mind and different preparation. So, don't assume anything about this work, especially that it will be difficult or that it's not for you (because you're too shy or you're afraid or you're only good at talking to your friends). Really, how do you know if you're any good at this until you've had a go at it?

Pace is personal, though. And 'fast' doesn't always mean 'bad'. Sometimes I think negative commentary on pace was invented by dysfunctional managers who just wanted to criticize other people's speaking. I hear from lots of women seeking to improve how they come across in public that they've been taught by coaches and consultants that they must and must not do certain things. (Don't cross your legs in a meeting. Don't speak too fast.) When we can see that there are so many different kinds of performance and leadership, why, then, do we think that women should behave in a certain way?

I've worked on voice coaching with women who have been specifically told by managers or colleagues to slow their speech. On closer examination, I've realized that their brain works really quickly and they have a lot of ideas to get out. Those speakers have to learn how to 'read' the audience and 'teach' themselves to adjust their pace, by listening and observing reactions. It's an extremely fine line and a very personal thing. It needs to be judged according to each situation. Is your audience following you? Can you see people nodding? Or frowning? Why are you talking fast? Does it enhance the audience's experience or make it more difficult for them?

Sometimes speakers talk fast because they feel pressure to over-deliver and they want to cram in everything they know on a topic. But a fifteen-minute presentation doesn't require you to download your entire brain. It requires you to introduce and develop three succinct, interesting talking points or conclusions. It could represent a fraction of a percentage of what you know about something. Maybe if someone is telling you to slow down, they are also saying you really don't need to try that hard. You can deliver less content and take your time.

Be prepared to get it wrong

The other great lesson to take from Virginia Woolf is her attitude to failure, which was extremely open. She recognized that it was necessary to go through a lot of self-doubt and self-examination before you could say anything that really mattered. It's perhaps no coincidence that the only surviving recording of her voice was from a BBC series entitled *Words Fail Me*. 'Words,' she says, 'like us to think, and they like us to tell, before we use them; but they also like us to pause; to become unconscious.' Her message is as much about the spaces between the words (for the audience to think about what she is saying and make their own associations) as it is about what she has written or said.

It takes a writer like her to show that there are, of course, many parallels between preparing for speaking events and writing. You have to be prepared to do it badly and improve on the job. This is high-stakes stuff. As the novelist Philip Roth said of his work: 'Over the years what you develop is a tolerance for your own crudeness. And patience with your own crap, really. Belief in your crap, which is just "stay with your crap and it will get better, and come back every day and keep going".' This is what you need in order to write fiction. But it's also what you need if you're committing to being a better communicator. What does Roth mean here by 'tolerance'? He means putting up with the fact that you won't always do it perfectly: you'll often make mistakes and sometimes embarrass yourself. If this is good enough for him and Virginia Woolf, it's got to be good enough for the rest of us.

Granted, this is more stressful with speaking than many other endeavours as you aren't able to camouflage your 'crap' simply by making sure it's never published. You will have to say the 'crap' out loud in public to see if it works. If novelists had to do this, there would probably be far fewer of them. I haven't done the exact maths but I suspect there are many thousands more novels published each year than there are people who attempt stand-up comedy for the first time. Which is interesting because it's a lot less effort to attempt stand-up comedy than it is to write a novel. See what I mean, though, about high stakes? We really are scared of failing in public. So much so that most people would rather spend three years writing a novel privately than do a five-minute stand-up set.

The trouble with the hang-ups many of us have about what I call 'scrutinized communication' (it's not much better than 'public speaking', is it?) is that we fear the outcome more than the process. Our fear feels similar to the adrenalin of the fight-or-flight response. For some people the fear is so great that they feel almost as if their life is in danger. In my experience, although the audience may be indifferent to you or sometimes outwardly hostile, no one will try to kill you. Not intentionally, anyway. As the American coach Brendon Burchard writes in *The Motivation Manifesto*: 'Almost all fear we experience today, and its resultant cowardly thinking and behaviour, is just imagined social drama created by unchecked mental processes and conditioning. We are afraid of being rejected, isolated or abandoned – not of being eaten alive.'

These unchecked fears are just like Virginia Woolf's Angel in the House, the voice inside telling us we shouldn't overstretch ourselves, others will judge us, and terrible things we can't even imagine will happen to us. 'My mind turned by anxiety, or other cause, from its scrutiny of blank paper, is like a lost child – wandering the house, sitting on the bottom step to cry,' writes Woolf.

We have to shake ourselves out of this and focus on the task in hand. We have to write the speech, book the speaking opportunity, get through it. And the way to do that is to channel Virginia Woolf: slow your pace, breathe, let yourself sink into it and enjoy it.

Tips and Tricks

— Your speed is highly determined by your breath. You ignore your breath at your peril! It's a great tool to use to keep yourself relaxed and to find natural pauses in your speech. Just a few moments spent thinking about your breathing before or at the beginning of a speech will relax you. Notice how you punctuate what you're saying using your breath. Other people need time to absorb thoughts and register what you've just said. When you take a breath, it gives them time to do that.

— Pace is often dictated by nerves, and nerves can also be controlled by the breath. If you're gabbling, register that and take a moment. Feel the soles of your feet on the floor; let your brain drop into your stomach; breathe through your feet. Relax. Pick up your thought and start again.

— If you have spoken for a while and suddenly realize it was too fast, have the guts to admit it and stop. Say, 'Let me give you a moment to take all that in.' Then take a couple of deep breaths and continue at a more easily understandable pace.

— Your pace is a big part of how you engage an audience. It's as much about how fast or slow you choose to go as it is about how much you are listening to them, watching them and registering if they are following you. As Virginia Woolf might have realized when she gave her lectures, at literary festivals there is often a direct correlation between how engaging a speaker is and how well their book sells afterwards. I'm not saying that the slower an author speaks, the more copies they'll sell, but I do advocate a close watch on audience engagement. (And, yes, I know that people fall asleep in literature festival audiences. It's the age demographic. You need to wake them up, perhaps by making others laugh.)

Exercises

— Make a recording of yourself on your phone, ideally talking at an event. If you don't have the opportunity to do that, then record a dummy sixty-second speech. Listen to it whenever you get a spare minute (on the train, etc.). On the one hand, this is good practice for getting used to hearing your own voice and analysing yourself. On the other, it's really useful for pacing. Are you speaking slowly enough? Are there parts where you could slow down or speed up? One of the most important elements of speaking is being able to hear yourself how others hear you and analyse objectively how you're coming across to an audience. Practice will help.

— The next time you're in a meeting, notice the pace of your own speech and that of others. Do people listen more when you slow down? Can you force yourself to speak uncomfortably slowly? What difference does that make?

— In a meeting, job interview or important conversation, have something in mind you would like to say in conclusion to a point or that you really want to drop in. Make it short and easy to remember. Practise saying it slowly and deliberately. In every conversation, we all have something we really want to get across; in more formal conversations we may throw it away or mumble it. Focus on what that thing is for you and resolve to say it slowly. Sometimes it's a question: 'So. When can I get an answer on that?'; 'Is that something we can agree on?'; 'Can you commit to that pay rise?' (Seriously. This is what Virginia Woolf would want.)

5

Be More Oprah: Time's Up, Dry Gums and the Power of Conviction

Show your passion, wisdom and experience

Oprah Winfrey is a fascinating example of the power of intense self-belief, cultivated and hard-won over many years. She has always been a great speaker and has had many break-out moments over the course of her career when she has succeeded in communicating a global message. However, the moment when she received the Cecil B. de Mille Award for Lifetime Achievement at the Golden Globe Awards in January 2018 was extraordinary. The speech went viral instantly and has had at least 10 million views on YouTube. Perhaps it was the full-length Atelier Versace black velvet gown. Perhaps it was the 'I'm-giving-a-serious-speech' effect of her cat's-eye glasses. Or perhaps it was the conviction that comes from fifty years of speaking your mind and, finally, not caring what anyone else thinks. (Clue: it was the last. I was joking about the other two. Although she did look amazing. And it's interesting to note when speakers do and don't wear glasses: they often add a hint of gravitas. I can't wear them on stage: I feel too much like Professor McGonagall.)

The content, of course, was in part what sold it: this

was one of the first significant public speeches by a woman since the rise of #MeToo and #TimesUp. Also, a year after Donald Trump's election to the presidency, no woman had really spoken against him with significant impact. Yes, many women had spoken at the women's marches in 2017, including Madonna and Gloria Steinem. (More on the latter coming up.) But these were all speeches given in front of a huge live audience with no proper audio or recording, and none had the impact the speakers might have desired. Clearly Oprah had decided that the Golden Globes platform was her chance to tackle these themes and she wanted to have as much impact as possible.

Setting content aside (and the content is terrific), this is a masterclass. It combines happy high status, presence and stately pacing. It has the extra quality of someone who can work a live audience but has also spent their life making television programmes and is comfortable in front of a screen. It works as well in the room as it does for viewers watching afterwards. It has the ideal combination of the personal and the universal, and Oprah lets this show in her delivery: this speech really means something to her, in terms of her own lifetime achievements and of what she wants it to represent for others – a landmark moment when black culture is celebrated. (She was the first black woman to be given this Lifetime Achievement Award.)

If you watch this speech, you can see from the moment that Oprah walks up to the stage to Reese Witherspoon, who is presenting the award, she embodies the idea of 'owning the room'. She moves slowly, at her own pace. She fully accepts the audience's applause and adulation with-out it overwhelming her. She thanks them several times for their standing ovation and has to find a way – elegantly – to get them to shut up and sit down. She says, 'OK, OK. Thank you, Reese.' It's like a teacher indicating to the class that it's time to settle down now. It works. People sit as she launches into her speech, using a pointy finger to indicate that it's time to listen: a lesson is coming. Oprah is brilliant at what I call 'signposting': the emotional and physical cues that show the audience how to behave. She gives them simply and powerfully.

'Look, I'm showing you: this is the bit where you should pay attention'

Oprah Winfrey is an expert at managing our attention span, manipulating our emotions and delaying gratifica-tion. She speaks slowly and deliberately, being careful not to rush her story. She uses hand gestures to punctuate her words and raise the suspense. There are moments of applause but she controls them completely, raising her hand to indicate that people should stop clapping: she's going on. (Notice how many speakers let the audience applaud until they want to stop: that is not owning the room. Oprah's behaviour says: 'I'm in charge, not you. I am stage-managing your applause.') There is great stillness and control in her body throughout this speech, which she delivers into a mic on a stand, not behind a podium. Away from a podium, you are more 'exposed' to the audience so they automatically lean into you.

She also includes a number of 'markers' in her speech to direct our attention and link her thoughts. 'Which brings me to this . . .'; 'What I know for sure . . .' These moments give us time to take in what she's talking about and give her time to breathe. She paces herself through this nine-minute speech, not allowing herself to get carried away when the audience gets excited.

There are two points where she wants the speech to lift and she doesn't let it peak early. She waits for the moment when she says 'Time's up', which she allows to fill the auditorium as people rise to their feet, repeating it twice as the applause grows. (A great example of what to do when you want to wait for applause to subside naturally instead of cutting it off: repeat yourself or wait in silence.) Note also how she increases the power of 'Time's up' by pushing her voice up as she says it. Then, just when it seems as if that were the peak of the speech, another comes: 'A new day is on the horizon.' She makes sure that she turns up the volume in this section, the political rallying cry of the speech. Having been low-key and at TV-presenter level until now, she goes into full evangelical-preacher mode to indicate how serious she is. It's quite a ride.

To experience Oprah Winfrey's formal speaking is very much to be in the presence of a modern-day preacher. This is someone who does not really need a microphone or a screen. This is someone who radiates strength, power and conviction from the core of her being, like Billy Graham on steroids. For younger readers, Billy Graham made his name as the world's first TV evangelist. He was a sort of religious YouTuber long before anybody started making vlogs. He could be a divisive figure but something about his manner was hugely compelling. In the US from the 1940s until his death in 2005, many years before YouTube and TED Talks, he was a major role model for public speaking. Whatever you think about evangelical Christianity, his style and magnetism are incredible. We saw a similar style from Bishop Michael Curry. It is very rare to experience this kind of speaking from someone who is not a religious figure and from a woman. That is where Oprah comes in.

How to show rock-solid conviction

The hallmark of this 'preacher' style is the ability to capture and maintain attention, sometimes for long periods. Oprah's calling card is extreme conviction. At her live events, she speaks unscripted for at least an hour. To be able to do this, she speaks from a place of certainty that few people can access, let alone successfully transmit to others. From her speech at the Golden Globes in 2018 to her iconic commencement speeches, Oprah's signature speaking power is the ability to project a solid, definite idea. She does this by maintaining extreme focus and strong eye contact. I think to some degree this is innate and some people just have it. But it's also the product of experience, extreme openness and the highest possible end of happy high status.

I experienced this up close when I went to the *O* magazine conference in Atlanta, Georgia, in October 2011. I was one of several hundred women in a room with Oprah as she gave an hour-long sermon (I can only describe it as a sermon) about how to access your power. (If the idea makes you shudder then [a] you would have hated the whole thing and [b] we cannot be friends.)

One of the most interesting things about her speech was that it made you go into an almost trance-like state. She was incredibly hypnotic, drawing the audience to her by maintaining a combination of extreme stillness and choreographed movement. She used her body to direct your attention to her in the most controlled way: when she was making difficult points (often when she was directly referencing God, which she rarely does on television but does at live events), she was absolutely still. At other points, when she was being more informal or making jokes, she allowed herself to move across the stage so that everyone in the auditorium felt as if they were a part of her speech. Once I had ascertained that there were no car keys

Sellotaped to the underside of my seat, I was transfixed. (On her TV show, Oprah once gave away a car to every single person in the audience. The keys were under the chairs.)

I remember two things very clearly. First, she managed to convey a complicated and controversial idea in a simple and clear way. 'I come from the source,' I can remember her booming voice saying in a very slow and deliberate way, 'and I will return to the source.' She said this in the way a preacher would say it in a gospel church: you could hear people in the audience swaying and murmuring, 'Mmm-hmmm,' in the same way that Oprah appeared to be doing when the preacher was performing at Prince Harry and Meghan Markle's wedding. The idea in itself was fascinating and difficult to convey outside the speech. She was saying that we are all born from the same place and we all go back to the same place, which means we are all equal and there's nothing special about any of us. But, at the same time, we are all capable of great things. (I know. I'm making it sound cheesy. But, believe me, it was mind-blowing.)

Second, directly after this moment (which felt like a truth-bomb long before anyone used the expression), she came to the end of her speech and did something extraordinary: she took off her shoes. They were high-heeled patent Louboutins, the red soles glinting in the stage lights. She could have done this at any moment during the speech and made the point she wanted to make. ('I'm just like you. Although I can afford these fancy shoes, boy, are they killing me.') As it was, the gesture underlined the message she was trying to convey: 'We all think we're fancy and special. We're not. We're just wearing fancy heels. And we can take them off any time we want.' It was also a moment of great intimacy, like seeing her without make-up or in a private space. Of course it was calculated and done for show. But it worked. This was how she sold conviction to the crowd: 'I'm the real deal. This is all real. This means everything to me. I am here for you.' I'm sure there are Oprah-haters out there who wouldn't buy this. And I'm sure Oprah is not for everyone. But I would defy you to see her live and not fall under the spell.

This is typical Oprah, occupying extreme happy high status. (I don't think there is any happier high status than Oprah.) Presence. Pace. (Oprah never speaks fast and during that speech she spoke extremely slowly and left long pauses at the end of her thoughts.) But her addition to the brilliant speaking oeuvre, her signature, if you like, is the moments of intimacy and risk that display her true conviction. The stuff about returning to the source, and the elemental, bombastic way she delivered it, could have come across as over the top. Instead she owned it and meant it. The business of bending down to remove her heels to show that she too – despite her millions – is still humble and can still walk barefoot in front of others: that could have been stagey and fake. But it was not an empty gesture for her: she did it because in her heart she really meant it.

There's a great lesson here. But I'm not saying it's an easy one to learn. You do not become Oprah overnight. (Oprah did not become Oprah overnight.) You do not become someone who can say the words 'I come from the source and I will return to the source' (and not have people laugh in your face) without having extreme conviction. And you don't get away with taking your Louboutins off on stage unless you've earned it.

What do powerhouse speakers do that makes them so special?

One of the reasons Oprah is able to speak with this kind of conviction at this level is partly her comfort in front of a crowd (which can only come with a great deal of experience), partly the rhetorical devices she uses (these can be learned) and partly her use of story (which she can now use in shorthand as her audience will usually be familiar with much of hers).

Let's look first at how she uses rhetorical devices. She asks a lot of questions of the audience. 'Do you know what I mean when I say . . .?'; 'Has anybody else ever felt that . . .?' She also makes direct appeals and refers to 'you' when she means 'I'. 'You know what I'm saying when I tell you . . .'; 'When you see something like that, you know what you have to do'; 'You know what I'm talking about.' It builds up the impression that this is a conversation between friends who have shared experiences. This is not her speech. It is 'our' speech.

If you watch footage of Oprah from twenty or thirty years ago, this style is something she has learned, honed and developed. Which is not to say that thirty years ago she wasn't a great broadcaster and interviewer: she always was. The 1980s fashions were often off-the-chart insane and sometimes make her look incredibly uncomfortable but what Oprah does very well is adapt her style to the moment. This is why she is an actor as well as a public figure. If it's appropriate for her to take a back-seat role, be the interviewer, ask the questions and step away, she can do that. If she needs to look presidential, lead and show extreme force, she can do that too. She is always very 'alive' to the moment and listening hard to her audience, whether it's one person or an entire room. When I saw her speak, I think the audience was around two thousand. I have never had the sensation so strongly with any other speaker that, yes, she really was speaking exclusively to me.

There are a lot of lessons to take from Oprah. Perhaps the most valuable one is exposure and perseverance. She became a great interviewer by doing a lot of interviews. There are probably very few people on the planet who have done as many hours of live television as she has. This means making mistakes, messing up in front of millions and getting up tomorrow to do it all again. So, certainly determination is a big factor in her speaking success. She has said that her greatest confidence comes from 'a willingness to be vulnerable'. And that is not something you can just stand up and do in front of people: it comes with experience. Vulnerability means being able to mess up in public, to admit your failures, to own and explore them. Oprah has made a career of this.

I have seen many times in speaking workshops that people are not comfortable with being vulnerable. It's one of the things that hold them back most in speaking. What if I mess up? What if people discover I'm an idiot? What if everyone thinks I'm as bad as I think I am?

What I try to do – gently – in group settings is demonstrate how much we like other people when they mess up. If you do something wrong (trip up on the way to the stage, drop the microphone, ask a stupid question) but you're comfortable with it, other people love it. That's not to say you should mess up on purpose, but be aware that we don't expect others to be perfect. So why do we expect ourselves to be perfect? What we don't like to see as an audience are people who beat themselves up for no reason. So you made a mistake, so what? So you repeated yourself. Big deal. Be relaxed about it and people will forgive you and even enjoy your performance all the more.

Don't be afraid to be over-the-top – and take risks

The other thing Oprah does to ramp up the sense of conviction and power we get from her is to employ stillness. She is not afraid to do this in an extremely dramatic – almost melodramatic, quasi-religious – way. She doesn't pace, she doesn't try to 'own' the stage by moving around. She 'owns' it by keeping her body as still as possible and letting us come to her. Her head movements are also quite minimal and deliberate. She doesn't maintain an extreme static pose (we would have to go to someone like Angela Merkel for that) but she is disciplined in the way that she moves her head and her hands. She uses them to direct our attention and to punctuate her points. I don't suggest she is thinking about any of this while she is speaking. (Although I would be very surprised if she doesn't rehearse a lot of her speeches, especially something like the Golden Globes one. At practice sessions, you can iron out any creases and find moments in your speech where you can use your hands for punctuation.) She eventually does all these things unconsciously because she is intimately connected with the words in her speech, the thoughts and the emotions behind them.

This is the quality of public speaking where it becomes – as with Michelle Obama – difficult for mere mortals to take lessons. Will any of us ever give a speech as meaningful as Oprah's when she was receiving a Golden

Globe, remembering when she saw Sidney Poitier winning one as her mother came home tired from her cleaning job? Or a speech like Michelle's, when she described what it's like to see her daughters grow up in the White House which was built by slaves?

It's unlikely any of us will ever have to give speeches on this level. But we can take risks in the way that Oprah Winfrey has taken risks. It looks easy for her now because she has amassed a vast fortune and has a great deal of power. But she has failed many times and admitted to a nervous breakdown in the early 2010s when her initial attempts to launch her own TV network failed. She has also talked about her performance anxiety when she had to push herself out of her comfort zone in acting roles. Of her role in *The Immortal Life of Henrietta Lacks*, she said, 'Every time I'm on stage I just feel like everybody here knows more than I do. So you have to then hand yourself over to somebody who knows what they're doing [i.e. the director] so that's what I did.' This is good advice. If you don't know what you're doing, put someone in charge who does.

Ahead of the Golden Globes speech, Oprah said afterwards, she had had an uncharacteristic attack of nerves. 'I must have been more nervous than I thought, because I've never had dry mouth before. In the middle of the speech, I thought, "I can't move my gums." I started to articulate because I was trying to get over my gums.' If you watch the speech back you cannot see this happening. Or if you can see her articulating, you think it's because she's passionate and wanting to really push her message. You don't think it's because of her gums. So the next time you get nervous and think you can't do something – or the next time you're in the middle of a speech and think your mouth has gone dry – remember Oprah, her gums and the 10 million views that speech has had. We hold ourselves to ridiculously high standards. We don't need to.

Tips and Tricks

— Obviously if you're trying to channel someone like Oprah or have a moment like hers at the Golden Globes, expectation management comes in handy. For a powerhouse performance like that, the setting and the aesthetic of the thing are very much part of the effect. Part of the impact of the Golden Globes speech was the response of the high-octane celebrities who were surrounding her (applauding, in tears, and rising to a standing ovation). Another part of it was her appearance: extreme high-status glamour. But there is no reason that you can't transplant those ideas into another setting. I've seen award-winners at very low-key (not black tie) ceremonies give life-changing speeches where they were able to articulate succinctly, briefly and emotionally why they did the work they did and why it should matter to others.

Picking a moment of success (the receipt of an award) is always a good moment to choose because people are already rooting for you and want to help you celebrate. If you can show them why it matters to you, you will create an electric speaking moment. Talk about a personal memory; tell the story of someone whose life was changed by your work; show your emotions about what you do. Don't avoid speaking about something that will make you emotional: the whole point is to choose something that you find difficult to talk about.

— There's no humour in Oprah's Golden Globes speech, intentionally. She has serious things to say and she doesn't want anything to undermine that. This doesn't mean it has to be heavy: she keeps in references to herself as a child and conjures up the image of her watching TV at home, staring up at the screen wide-eyed. Anything you can do to bring in personal 'pictures' that the audience can see in their mind's eyes will create warmth and empathy.

— If you are going to appeal to the audience to join you ('And their time is up!'), you have to be prepared to sell your idea: you can't wimp out. If Oprah's voice had dropped on the 'Time's up' line, the entire speech would have fallen flat. If you're going to ask people in a speech to care about something, to make a donation, to change their behaviour, make sure you mean it – and indicate it with a rise in your voice, both in tone and volume.

Exercises

— Make a list of ten things you really care about. It could be stuff you care about in your everyday life or subjects linked to your work. Don't overthink it. Write the ten things as quickly as possible and don't judge yourself if some of them seem silly.

— Pick the three you most care about and decide which you care about enough to write a speech on. It doesn't have to be a long speech. It doesn't even have to be a written speech. It could be something you say five sentences about as a vote of thanks at an event or talk about for one minute at an awards ceremony or office party. It could be something you could record for social media above a link for a charity giving page.

— Once you've chosen your one thing, write down five – 'And their time is up!' – phrases that suit your subject. It may be something like: 'And that's why I need your help'; 'This means the world to me'; 'We have to do something now before it's too late'; 'Believe me: you need to act'; 'If I can persuade you of one thing, it's to give whatever you can right now.'

— Commit to giving this speech somewhere and give yourself a deadline. You could record it and put it out on social media in the next week. You could go on Facebook Live in the next twenty-four hours. You could ask your boss if you can give a vote of thanks at her leaving party. These opportunities don't come unless you create them. (Unless you wait for your Golden Globes

Lifetime Achievement Award. But even then, when you get it, that speech will be better if you've practised with smaller versions.)

6

Be More Joan: The Value of Authenticity, Not Caring and Embracing Your Own Obnoxiousness

You don't have to be likeable to be a good speaker

There's an online video from 2014 billed 'Joan Rivers' last appearance'. She's talking into a television camera outside what looks like an airport. But she doesn't talk like a normal person being interviewed outside an airport. She talks like Joan Rivers. So although she's not on stage, she might as well be. The hallmarks? Every word and expression is magnified and exaggerated. She opens up her whole face, her eyes, her mouth. She uses extreme gestures: hands on hips, shoulders shrugging, arms held wide in a 'What fresh hell is this?' expression. Maybe not how you'd like to address your postman if you were saying good morning. And maybe not how you'd like to present a six-month forward-planning strategy if you'd just joined a new team. But effective nonetheless. And worth $150 million by the time of her death in 2014.

This kind of behaviour is certainly one way to command attention. But you need to be disciplined in how you use these moves: if you watch Rivers, she uses her arms to make her points but the rest of her body is still. It's not unlike Oprah but with more anger, more rudeness and more energy. The anger and the energy are contained and controlled, and deployed exactly how Rivers wants them deployed. And the rudeness is just Joan. What she's saying is outrageous and controversial (in this video she's talking about Israel). But it is a performance of outrage and a measured one, designed to get you to listen. Not everyone would be willing to use Joan Rivers's tactics to get attention. But there are things to be learned. And I mention the money, by the way, not to be vulgar but to foreground her success in case anyone is thinking, But I never even liked Joan Rivers. The point is to find different options in behaviour for different kinds of women. To show that anyone can do it. Rivers found the style that suited her and it was highly effective. As the comedian Sarah Millican says, 'Comedy is subjective. Success is objective.'

Although to me she is a wonderful role model for idiosyncrasy and doing things your own way, I have to admit that Joan Rivers is a great example of someone many other women would absolutely hate to emulate in any way whatsoever. Even a lacklustre performance by her (not that I'm suggesting she ever gave one) would be delivered with dynamism, verve, nervous energy and a level of vitriol that few women (or indeed persons of any gender) would be comfortable putting across. In many people's minds, Rivers is almost a stereotype of a stand-up comedian: brash, terrifying, irreverent, careless, rude, nasty, almost obscenely confident. These are not things many of us are comfortable to be and certainly not in public. Rivers said she was a great actress, doing a flawless impression of a stand-up comedian. Whatever she did, it was supposed to be larger than life and it was not necessarily supposed to be likeable. But it was always authentic. It was true to her.

That is why Joan Rivers is a great role model for other women. Although she was clearly a natural comedian, it wasn't as if she just walked on stage and did what she did. Thousands of hours of thought, preparation and failure went into her act. In the documentary *Joan Rivers: A Piece of Work*, we see her going through the famous filing cabinets in her office, which contained hundreds of thousands of index cards on hundreds of subjects, under titles like 'ugly', 'dumb', 'showbiz'. She worked exceptionally hard to build up that collection of words and ideas into a Rolodex in her head. She knew that somewhere in her filing cabinets she had a joke on everything, which could be crafted into a new set for any occasion. The work that goes into that is unimaginable. (And she did not do it alone: over the years she had many people writing for her.) But, more importantly, it is achievable if you set your mind to it. Surely that is more inspiring than thinking she just got up on stage and behaved like that. Or that she wrote everything herself. Rivers is proof that we all need help, we all need discipline and we all need a huge amount of practice. It takes a lot of work to be that successful at being funny.

Do whatever it takes, even if it means 'cheating'

Even more inspiring and useful for anyone wanting to find their own voice, Joan Rivers had to learn how to 'cheat' and fake it, as many performers do. This didn't make her any less professional. I saw her perform several times at the Royal Albert Hall in the years before she died, and even in the cheapest seats you could see the giant cue cards carefully taped across the front of the stage. Did anyone care or notice? Of course not. Did anyone who had paid top dollar for a ticket mind or complain? Of course not. It wasn't even that they forgave her, or thought, Oh, she needs the cue cards – she is seventy-nine years old, after all. Her performance was on such a level and she was so relaxed with her own needs on stage that very few in the audience would even have registered it. That is a fantastic lesson to learn. She would rather take the help than not perform.

This illustrates a piece of advice from Jennifer Palmieri, who was Hillary Clinton's director of communications during her election campaign. She also worked in the White House for Barack Obama. In her book *Dear Madam President*, she writes about the tip she received from Bill Clinton's press secretary, Evelyn Lieberman: 'People take their cue from you. That's it. If you act like you belong in the room, people will believe you do. If you act like your opinion matters, others will too.' However you behave on stage, however you enter a room, whatever expectations you give to people, they will take that at face value. Joan Rivers did not make a big deal of using cue cards and didn't seem to be remotely irritated that she needed them. She accepted them as a necessity and concentrated on the performance. That is extremely gutsy.

The same goes for the index cards and that enormous filing cabinet. (Seriously. Watch the documentary. It fills an entire wall of an office. That is decades' worth of work.) Some people might think of that as a formulaic way to approach material or even see it as a bit disappointing that a woman with an extraordinarily wild and free manner on stage required that academic level of organization to be able to deliver. To me, this is in itself extremely liberating: to know that you can find a system that works for you and stick to it. And to know that electric, jaw-dropping performances do not come out of nowhere. They can be broken down into dozens of index cards, memorized many times over, worked up and corrected until they are filed away, only to come back years later to be worked on and remembered again. This is the great myth of performance that so many of us have swallowed: that it comes effortlessly and you need to be born Joan Rivers to be Joan Rivers. You do a bit, of course. But you also need to do the work.

Take an attitude towards criticism: either embrace it or ignore it

Joan Rivers was relentlessly hard on herself and recognized the importance of taking a stance on reviews of her performances. I think it's fine to solicit criticism and read reviews. And it's fine not to. The one thing you shouldn't do is let other people's views creep up on you when you're not ready for them. Either make a concerted effort to ignore criticism or take it on board in an organized way. Not only was Joan Rivers the ultimate grafter, terrified by the thought of white space in her diary, but she also adopted a brutal approach to criticism, staying abreast of it and registering it, even if it was painful.

Many comedians, performers and writers avoid criticism and actively shun reviews, good or bad. Good reviews, so the argument goes, make you believe the hype and become self-conscious. Bad reviews make you hate yourself and want to give up. There's a whole school of thought about how to deal with them and Rivers wanted to know everything, good or bad. The bad reviews were fuel for her. If people didn't get her or were harsh on her or thought she should give up, she used it: 'I'll show you.' At the same time, she paid a price for this.

In the documentary, we see an assistant reading a review to her from the paper. It's not good and Rivers is visibly crushed. She rarely seemed to enjoy her success and nothing was ever enough for her: the higher she climbed, the more critics there were. Certainly she took some satisfaction in the material rewards of her work (this was a woman who had wall-to-wall leopard-print carpet in her multi-million-dollar apartment) but she was still working like a demon right up to her death. She died on the operating table, the place where she had spent so much time making the changes that were designed to keep her in business for as long as possible.

The argument against holding up Joan Rivers as a role model is that many women will think, But I'm nothing like her. And I wouldn't want to be anything like her. It doesn't help that Rivers herself – whether for real or publicity purposes – was a self-declared anti-feminist, who railed against the younger women who were not grateful enough for the trail she had blazed and who knew that her audiences came to see her not because she was sisterly, sweet and generous but because she was a total bitch (and I mean this in a nice way). In reality, though, Rivers's self-actualization was the most feminist act: she didn't measure herself against anyone else, she became the performer only she could be; she fought tooth and nail for the most advantageous fees for herself. Her life and performance may not be obvious or even sensible things to copy. But the spirit of it all is wildly inspirational.

Life lessons from stand-up comedy (yes, there are some)

Shortly after I started out in comedy, I mentioned stand-up to Dame Judi Dench, when I was lucky enough to be inter-viewing her for a magazine. I expected her to nod sagely and say, 'Oh, yes, I tried that once. I was quite funny.' Instead her eyes popped out of her head at the idea and she looked terrified just thinking about it: 'My God, girl, you've got some guts.' She said she would never think of doing it because it was completely terrifying. She's right. Stand-up comedy takes pure guts. Lucille Ball used to say: 'I'm not funny. I'm brave.'

No one had more guts than Joan Rivers. She pushed herself on stage in a way few female performers have ever done and at a time when no one else was doing it. Her speaking style is about using all the things voice coaches and directors will tell you not to use: fast speech, shouting, pushing your voice until you're hoarse, moving around a lot on stage, using your hands wildly. Stand-ups like Rivers teach us about using the rules so that they can be broken: how to make it work for you. There are a lot of things about her that you should not want to emulate (including her cas-ual racism). But there is a huge lesson in finding your own path, working it out for yourself, ignoring what everyone else is doing, and not bothering about being likeable.

When I see much younger women complaining about

sexism and the odds they face (I'm not saying that their perception is wrong), I often think of Joan Rivers and her extreme unwillingness to portray herself as a victim. When she went into stand-up, she was stigmatized, not just by audiences and many people she was working alongside but also by society and her family, who did not approve of what she was doing. Later, she was dropped from her television show. Her husband committed suicide. And she had to dig herself out of a multi-million-dollar debt hole left to her by his death and a business swindle. That is serious pressure. Rivers never gave up. She barely blinked. She just continued working like a demon into her eighties. I don't want to say that in terms of a life lived there is necessarily something positive to emulate here. If you watch the documentary about her life, Rivers comes across as an extremely unhappy person who lost herself in her work because otherwise she couldn't bear to live. But in terms of taking your identity and your success from your career and bashing people over the head with the strength of your personal belief until they get on board, her example can't be beaten.

Many of the lessons I've learned about public speaking are taken from stand-up comedy. That's partly because this is the world I know. But it's also because I think understanding the (unhelpful and often inaccurate) perceptions we have about stand-up comedy can be useful, particularly to women. Women are still grossly under-represented in comedy and many are biased against trying it. Yes, men can be nervous of stand-up too, but not to the same extent. Once we see that there are different ways of thinking about something that seems 'scary', we can apply it to other situations. It's not that you have to have an interest in stand-up or ever want to do it. It's just that the message from stand-up is transferable. The lessons from it – painfully learned by others without you ever having to tell a joke that falls flat – can help with your own speaking.

For me, it was profoundly liberating to find out that stand-up comedians – and, yes, even Joan Rivers – are just as scared of speaking as any other person may be. Even household names, appearing on television programmes they've been doing for years, struggle with nerves, physical tics, dry mouth, trembling hands and self-doubt. These things are not individual to any of us. They are the collective human experience. People who choose to speak publicly, speak well and devote their lives to perfecting it don't necessarily do it because it's easy for them or they never suffer when they're in that position. They do it in spite of and alongside that. They accept that it is human to feel these things and they get on with the job.

Also, many of the situations that stand-up comedians face have a direct parallel even in the most staid corporate environments. If I'm coaching someone to speak at a very serious conference where the speaker wants to connect with the audience, we will rehearse 'fake' eye contact (sweeping the room without actually catching anyone's eye) and practise imagining the front row and what you will do if someone (a) appears sleepy and bored (b) looks like they hate you or (c) seems completely disengaged from what you're saying. These are all things you have to learn in stand-up.

You also have to learn extreme resilience. Joan Rivers was the queen of bouncing back from rejection and refusing to go away. All stand-ups have to learn this. It's part of the job. Any audience can reject you at any moment. Constant knockbacks are part of the career path. *New York* magazine once published a tenth-anniversary collection by Mindy Tucker, who photographs comedians on the New York scene. She asked the subjects to look at pictures of themselves from a decade ago and say what they would now tell the person in the photograph. Their responses are fascinating. 'Don't let the ups and downs stay all cooped up in your head – give 'em a little breathing room'; 'Go to therapy, be weird and don't dwell on things too much'; 'You're doing fine. Be patient. Be kind. Keep at it'; 'It's gonna get really hard, especially one night in 2009 that you won't think you'll rebound from. You will'; 'Cry a bit more and think a little less'; 'I thought comedy was only worthwhile if it felt difficult, and the audience could see that effort'; 'Anxiety is your creativity turned into a weapon that you use to beat yourself up.'

You see? Even people who are tough suffer and find

this difficult. It's normal. Just because something is difficult, it doesn't mean you're not meant to do it.

But . . . why stand-up is not like other speaking situations

The other important thing to bear in mind when you're giving a speech is context. Very often it is not acknowledged at work events that the speaker is set up in a position to fail or where, at the very least, they are pushing a boulder uphill. In stand-up comedy and in the theatre, many conventions exist to give the performers the best chance. They are beautifully lit in a theatre or a comedy club, which makes them easy to focus on (and, often, look more attractive than they are in harsher light – and we all find it easier to focus on someone who is attractive). They are not plonked in front of some shonky podium with no lighting, no sound check and no one to announce who the hell they are. Joan Rivers would not have appeared on stage in those conditions, I'm sure.

In a theatre, the audience is primed into submission. There are warnings about switching off your mobile phone. They are in darkness so (a) they relax because they feel unseen and unscrutinized, and (b) the performer cannot see them properly, if at all, which prevents distraction. The performance is properly delineated (a curtain goes up, someone gives a proper introduction, the lights are dimmed).

In work situations, these things don't happen. Or someone might try to make them happen a bit, which almost makes it worse.

When work environments set things up for speaking, it's hardly *Live at the Palladium*. You're probably in some ante-room with strip lighting and a boardroom table. And you're supposed to hold people's attention for up to thirty minutes? I have been asked to give advice to speakers about how they can command more attention during a presentation because some of their colleagues fall asleep or check their phones. The only answer I can give is that they have to change the context (get people to hand in their mobile phones, make sure the meeting is held at a time of day when no one is inordinately tired or has just made a long journey, get a better room . . .).

If a bunch of actors walked into a pub and suddenly started performing scenes from Shakespeare, would you pay any attention, if you were out for a drink with a group of friends? Of course not. You'd probably wish they'd go away. Can you imagine what Joan Rivers would do if someone was using their phone in the front row at a performance? Or if they fell asleep? But you can't react in the same way at work.

Unfortunately, though, in work contexts, people rarely acknowledge these drawbacks. This leads to the wrong expectations. Too many people arrange a speaker event at work and expect it to be on the level of a TED Talk or even close to stand-up comedy. Unless you've set it up with the same production values, that in itself is a joke. To organize a meeting or a speaker event with no regard for production values, no regard for the audience's attention span and no regard for the feelings of the speaker . . . It won't be great. I'm not suggesting you have to make a Hollywood production of everything but you do need to be realistic. If you've set up a room where people are free to wander in and out, attention will be only half on the speaker. If you've set up a presentation where the most senior person comes in fifteen minutes late and slumps into a half-doze, no one will focus on what is being said. If you're on a video conference call and have your hair all over your face and are constantly looking down, no one is going to listen to you. This is pretty basic stuff. But for some reason we forget it.

On the one hand, I'd like to see people do something about this culture and change it. On the other, I'd like them to acknowledge it so that they understand companies often have unrealistic expectations of speakers – and individuals often have unrealistic expectations of themselves. This can be incredibly helpful when you're in a speaking situation: 'This is unwinnable. The context is all wrong. The most I can do is my best and just get it over with.' You can't rent the Royal Albert Hall as Joan Rivers would have done or put on a sequined blazer for your boss's leaving party (although please send me a picture if you do), but you can institute clear boundaries in work settings to make your speaking easier.

I heard about one of the best outcomes I've ever had after a corporate training session when, a year later, one of my class came back and said, 'I've banned phones from meetings and events, and things have improved massively.' She hadn't previously wanted to make this request in meetings in case she was seen as too forceful or domineering. Or in case her request was disregarded, which would have undermined her authority. But sometimes you just have to ask yourself, 'What would Joan Rivers have done?' (She would have thrown everyone's phone into the sea.)

Don't be afraid to be a bitch

In terms of public speaking and 'showing up', Joan Rivers is also a great example because she defies many conventions women are taught to accept in order to 'come across better' in public. According to conventional wisdom, she speaks way too fast. She speaks seemingly with a lack of clarity: she splutters, stutters, restarts bits. She is crude, says difficult or socially unacceptable things, paints herself as a harridan, makes herself into a hate figure, contorts her face into ugly expressions . . . I could go on. OK, so these are conventions of comedy and you couldn't get away with any of it if you were a female politician or 'serious' business leader. But her exuberant mannerisms are important because early in her career, to see a woman behaving like that – whether it's 'serious' or not – defied norms. (And, fascinatingly, they still do. I think that a comedian like Joan Rivers now would cause all kinds of problems for people by being so brash and blunt, especially as a woman. She absolutely hated political correctness and I wonder if now she would even have a career in the current climate.)

She was also a great example of why you shouldn't listen to received wisdom. Everything in the culture surrounding Joan Rivers would have told her it was a bad idea to follow the path she did, not only in her career but also in terms of how she remade her face and body repeatedly. She was ridiculed many times for her stage act and for her looks. This hurt her but it did not deter her because she saw that alongside all the critiques and hate came success. In fact, the more criticism and hatred there was, the higher her star rose. I'm convinced this fuelled her plastic surgery. It gave her a career by keeping her in the headlines and by making sure that people were always interested in what she looked like, even if it was to say that she was a mess. The path she chose to success was rather perverted, then, but it was also lucrative and it gave her the limelight she craved up to the age of eighty-one. I cannot think of a single other performer in her field who created the same kind of opportunities for herself.

The other extraordinary thing about Joan Rivers is that none of this came easy to her. Yes, she had the raw material to make herself into the performer she became, but she had a ton of obstacles in her way from the very beginning. For me one of the main lessons of Joan Rivers's life is the benefit of aligning your own identity with your career. She clearly felt that she was no one without her life on stage. She was never someone who was going to retire and spend more time with friends. She was only really able to have a good relationship with her daughter by working on screen with her. There's something tragic about that. But it's also inspirational: she recognized her own weirdnesses, eccentricities and limitations and built a life that accommodated them. This isn't for everyone but it's a fantastic lesson in self-knowledge.

If ever you find yourself thinking, Well, it was easy for someone like Joan Rivers. She must just have had loads of guts and have been naturally outspoken . . . remember what she was going through when she was having meetings about TV and showing up on stage to make jokes when her husband had just taken his life. She is proof that if you put your mind to something you can make it happen, regardless of how many difficulties might spring up. She did love to kvetch and bitch about how hard she had to work and how under-appreciated she was, but she also loved to downplay her success and make out that in some ways she had found the easy route: 'I've succeeded by saying what everyone else is thinking.' Ah, if only it were that easy . . .

Tips and Tricks

— Be honest with yourself about what sort of person you are. Often I see people who are not corporate people trying to force themselves into corporate roles. Do you think Joan Rivers would have been good at delivering a PowerPoint presentation on next year's marketing targets? Of course not. (Although I would have liked to see this.) If you realize this is happening to you, it doesn't mean you're in the wrong job and need to give everything up to become a stand-up comedian or a cruise-ship singer. It just means you need to acknowledge that, right now, you're discharging speaking opportunities that are not 100 per cent in alignment with who you are as a person. Use it as an opportunity to push the limits, see how much of yourself you can put into work presentations and just practise connecting with an audience. Also, think about where you really want to be and what would suit you better. Starting to work out what kind of speaker you'd like to be can be challenging: if you want to speak strongly, honestly and openly from the heart, it will be hard to do that meaningfully if you're in a job you hate. Be gentle with yourself: remember that we can all change something and you don't have to do it overnight.

— We need people who are not ideally suited to certain work environments to shake things up. If it feels fake to you to put on certain presentations in which people always fall asleep or meetings where no one pays attention (I hear about this all the time), can you talk to someone about it? What can you do to make these interactions more meaningful? This is where your authenticity comes in.

— Don't beat yourself up if sometimes you have to toe a line for a contribution to be appropriate. Work set-ups are not designed for life-changing song-and-dance numbers so set your expectations accordingly.

Exercises

— If you're preparing for a speech, challenge yourself to put a joke in at the end and at the beginning. It can either be a short funny story about something that happened to you and is relevant, a saying that makes you laugh or a quote on that topic from someone famous – Google is your friend here. (Type in, for example: 'Ryan Gosling interview quotes'.) Or you can use a line from a fictional character in a movie: 'As the great actor Ryan Gosling once asked four times in the seminal movie *The Notebook*, "What do you want?" ' You have to be able to style this out if people don't laugh. (And, boy, did I struggle to find a Ryan Gosling quote, whether from real life or on-screen. I ended up with one that wasn't very good. He hasn't said much that's of use. Maybe google Helen Mirren instead. The point is to choose someone you find inspiring or entertaining and have fun.)

— One of the biggest lessons to take from Joan Rivers is about developing your own sense of self-belief. The best exercise I know for this is to take a pen and a piece of paper. Set a timer for two minutes. Write down ten things about yourself that make you proud. It can be anything from: 'I gave birth with no drugs.' (That's mine. Not showing off. Just a fact.) To: 'I managed to get up this morning.' (Also me. But only just.) 'I won an award for my great work with orphans.' (This is not me.) And: 'I won a BAFTA.' (Not just yet.)

When your two minutes are up, read through your ten things and allow yourself to feel pride. Now set your timer for twenty minutes and write another forty things on that list to get the number up to fifty. Go as fast as you can. Mine every single small moment of pride you've ever felt. It's hard to get to fifty but force yourself. When you're done, keep hold of this list and take it everywhere with you. Read it when you're experiencing self-doubt. I have no proof that Joan Rivers did this but most of the time she acted as if she was carrying around ten volumes of her greatest achievements.

7

Be More JK: The Commencement Speech and the Importance of Your Personal Story (with Help from Ellen DeGeneres and Amal Clooney)

You don't have to be a great speaker to give an amazing speech

Some of the best viral speeches of recent years have been commencement speeches. Or, as Ellen DeGeneres calls them, 'common cement' speeches. This is what American universities call the speeches given on graduation day when they invite an outsider to tell the students how to 'commence' the rest of their lives. Usually these come from people who don't regularly give speeches in public – and who probably had to have their arm twisted to speak at all. Even if they are performers (and Jim Carrey has given a brilliant one), this is the moment when they can't hide behind a celebrity persona or an act. It is a version of them that is stripped back to the essentials: 'This is who I am. And this is what I think you need to help you live the rest of your life.' The best are often very raw and touching.

Commencement speakers are worth studying not just because of what they're talking about. They illustrate the fact that you don't have to be a speaker as your day job to be a good one. All you have to do is talk about what you know in a way that is approachable and engaging. Just as many of the best TED Talks have come from people who are writers, scientists or academics, these speeches are not about showcasing brilliant speaking *per se*. In fact, they often contradict a lot of the ideals about brilliant speaking. Commencement speeches usually allow for reading from a script (which doesn't happen at TED, although some speakers seem to use autocue as back-up) and for hesitation or stumbling. It doesn't have to be perfect. But it does have to be a piece of storytelling that shows something of the person giving the speech. If you're Ellen DeGeneres, you can get away with doing this in a bathrobe. I can't see anyone else styling it out in quite the same way.

Part of the charm of the commencement speeches that have done well online is their content. What does this person think it takes to live a good life? But none would work if they weren't delivered with awareness that the speaker has something important to impart: what they've lived through. The best commencement speeches are flawed in their delivery. They're emotional. They're sometimes surprising. Often they're by a comedian who does not say anything funny. They're about keeping it real and showing people you can do something that is out of your professional milieu.

J. K. Rowling is one of the best examples of this. She speaks rarely in public. But when she does, it's impactful. It needs to be. She's J. K. Rowling and people expect her to be amazing. But think about the burden that represents:

she has chosen to live her life squirrelled away, writing books. Do you think she likes the idea of putting on a silly hat and a university gown and telling people how to live a good life? I doubt it. Yet she does it with grace and ease. With a little reluctance, which we can sense, yes, but that only adds to the authenticity and the feeling that this is a gift. She's overcoming her own reluctance about giving this speech to say something important.

Show them who you really are

One of the things the audience is hoping for at a commencement speech by a famous person is an insight into their lives away from the spotlight. They want a glimpse of the inner person. They want a flavour of what it has felt like to be on their journey. In some ways, they want to feel as if they have sat next to that person at a dinner party. J. K. Rowling nailed this during her speech at Harvard Commencement in 2008. It soon became the most watched speech on their website and was eventually so successful that its contents were published as a book.

The audience wants to see how you respond to them genuinely in the moment. Someone else clearly gives a cue for the applause to stop. With her status (and she is not very happy high status although she is high status), Rowling does the right thing to self-deprecate at the beginning. The audience loves her so much without her having to say anything and they love her all the more when she says, essentially, 'I'm just like you. I didn't want to give this speech.' The form with commencement speeches is that the speaker can choose whether to read a text, memorize their words or ad lib. J. K. Rowling reads from a script. She's so appealing and warm that we forgive her immediately for this. (I say 'forgive' because I think a speech is always stronger if it can be delivered without notes.)

She then says that she based her speech on another commencement speech she heard – of which she can't remember a word. 'This liberating discovery', she says, allowed her to write freely because she realized that whatever she said everyone would forget it instantly. What's interesting about her in this moment is that she is so controlled. She allows the jokes to work slowly and waits for people to get them. She doesn't rush and she doesn't laugh at her own jokes.

Perhaps one of the most powerful things about this speech, though, is that she is visibly enjoying it. She says she hates it and didn't want to give it but this is clearly not true. She retreats into her paper many times, never losing concentration, occasionally misspeaking and stumbling, never losing anyone's attention. Another great reminder that you don't have to be perfect to give a perfect speech.

What's really vital to note about the speech, though, is that it succeeds mostly because J. K. Rowling is telling J. K. Rowling's story in her own words: that in and of itself is fascinating. If someone without her background and success told a similar story, it would not be so compelling. In fact, we would probably very quickly be bored by it. (Imagine a writer you've never heard of who has not sold many books telling you about how they struggled in the beginning. It's not going to go viral.)

This is an issue, I realize, with many of the speakers in this book and it's truly worth remembering: most of the examples we have of great speeches, whether by men or women, are by people who already hold a certain position in society, talking about their stories or saying what they think. They don't have to do the work of winning us over. And they don't have to do much to make us interested in them. We're already interested in them for who they are. Mostly, all they have to do is not be rubbish. That's an important lesson in expectation management. And it's also a reminder that we would all do well to look around for examples of brilliant speeches by people who don't have J. K. Rowling's advantage. It's great to look at these powerhouse speeches and be inspired by them, but perhaps even more inspiring is Janine from Accounts giving a PowerPoint presentation that makes everyone sit up and take notice. Time to take notes on how she achieved the effect.

It's OK to be a 'good-enough speaker'

J. K. Rowling does not have any theatrics in this speech or any Oprah-style 'Time's up' moment. She reads the speech she wrote. There is even a sense that her speaking would work just as well on the radio as it does face to face. And that is not the ideal speech, is it? There's very little drama or engagement. But she's an example of someone whose content is way more important than the delivery. That's understandable: she's a writer. Nonetheless there is a lesson to be learned from her tone: she is sincere, measured, fairly neutral, always humble, letting the words of the speech carry more resonance than a dramatic performance. Her tone matches the words perfectly, as she says: 'We touch other people's lives simply by existing.' All she has to do is say the speech with no bells and whistles.

When I say this kind of speech doesn't have to be perfect, take a look at Amal Clooney's commencement speech at Vanderbilt University in 2018. What does she do well? She speaks slowly and deliberately, checking in with the audience to make sure they're understanding her. She's clear and confident. She uses hand gestures to punctuate her points.

What does she do that isn't so great? She's reading from a script. At times she appears distracted and aloof. Her manner is more suited to a courtroom (where she would usually be speaking) than to an audience of students, who want to see something of the human being behind the professional façade. She fiddles with her hair, which is falling in her face, and she lets it conceal part of her face for some of the audience. If you're sitting on the right-hand side, you can hardly see her expressions. This is one of my cardinal sins of speaking: let people see your face. Don't have your hair over it. (At Harvard Commencement 2015, Natalie Portman, standing outside in a breeze, realizes this and tucks her hair behind her ears.)

Despite notable successes, the commencement speech is another example of a time when a speaker can be on a hiding to nothing. It's very difficult to make those speeches into a knockout, blow-you-away moment if you're not J. K. Rowling. You're trapped behind a podium. It's difficult to know which option to take: prepared or memorized speech. It needs to be largely aimed at students but mustn't alienate teachers or parents. It's a tough crowd and a tough gig. Even performers who are high energy and embrace risk on a regular basis tend to bow to the format of giving a prepared speech to be read aloud.

But you don't have to. You can do your own thing. Ellen DeGeneres at Tulane University Commencement in 2009 shows this. This is the second speech she gave here: at the first she wore the bathrobe. The man introducing her gives a great, warm introduction with no notes and with jokes. The camera pans to Ellen and she is visibly nervous. (Again, a great illustration of how It. Never. Goes.

Away. Do you believe me now? Even Ellen.) She gets up on stage, wearing a ridiculous academic gown. She keeps pulling at the neck of it because it's hot and uncomfortable. She talks direct to the audience, leaning over the podium. She has clearly written and learned this speech because it's full of thoughts and ideas that link one to the next. It's fascinating to see what she does when she gets a big laugh: 'I didn't go to college, and I'm not saying that you wasted your time or your money, but look at me, I'm a huge celebrity.' She waits it out. She doesn't smile or look pleased for herself. She just waits it out. Like J. K. Rowling, she tells her personal story, which is only really interesting because it's Ellen's story. (But it's a bloody good one.) At the end she goes and dances in the audience. I don't necessarily recommend this but it's a very Ellen thing to do and it works for her.

But back to J. K. Rowling, the mother of all commencement speech-makers. It's hardly surprising that the real reason her speech succeeds is because she tells stories, some of them personal. In fact, she interweaves several stories. Some we may already know (she started out as a failure). Some we may know less about (she used to work for a human-rights charity). She maintains a clever balance between her own stories and ours, always linking back to the students who are watching and the life journey they are about to start. She makes it clear that she has thought about a lot of their anxieties and shared the same worries herself. But she also pulls away into her own story to share her wisdom and experience, describing the meeting she had with a refugee who had just received terrible news about his family but who still had the presence of mind to be gracious, charming and polite to her. It has always stayed with her. This is a great illustration of how you don't have to find some grandstanding point or describe a historic meeting: you can just recall a human moment that really meant something to you and tie it in with the rest of your story. J. K. Rowling linked it to the idea that she has experienced failure and knows what really matters in life: truth and kindness. The small things are enough.

Be yourself: you can't be anyone else

It's interesting to contrast the poise of this Harvard speech with other J. K. Rowling appearances. She is not a regular speech-maker, as you can tell from the very few films online of her speaking. One of the few other examples of her public appearances is a very different kind of speech that she gives at the premiere for *The Deathly Hallows Part II*: she speaks informally and off the cuff to a huge crowd in Trafalgar Square. If you look at both speeches side by side, though, you see that the one thing J. K. Rowling is not afraid of (even if she doesn't like speaking) is being seen for who she is. She manages a formal situation at Commencement by writing a pitch-perfect speech. She manages an informal situation at the film premiere simply by being herself in circumstances she finds overwhelming.

At the premiere she is already crying when she starts speaking, clearly having absorbed the lesson that it's a good idea to 'be present' and 'be with us how you are'. She is fairly comfortable with her tears and allows herself to go with the emotion. (This is good.) For someone who clearly doesn't like speaking (I'm guessing this by the references she has made to her nerves and from the fact that she does it rarely), she is extremely at ease with a microphone here and works the crowd effortlessly. The interesting thing about this speech is that she doesn't have any content other than to thank everyone who has been involved in the Harry Potter films and this isn't fantastically interesting. (Sorry, J. K., I'm not blaming you. It's what you had to do in the circumstances.)

She also spoils the illusion of her own poise by saying, 'Grrr. Calm down,' to herself in the middle of the speech, which is completely unnecessary as she is doing a great job. And then she has to correct herself as she says initially that the director made three Harry Potter films when in fact he made four. But although this outing is slightly shambolic and almost feels as if it's happening under duress, she has clearly prepared a few lines that she is not going to forget: 'No story lives unless someone wants to listen.' And: 'Hogwarts will always be there to welcome you home.' This is a fantastic trick if you know you have to face a speech in unpredictable circumstances: have an opening line (or decide to ad lib something funny or just acknowledge a truth like 'This is very emotional for me and I can barely speak'), a middle line and an end line.

The one about Hogwarts is J. K. Rowling's closing line. These lines are great 'anchors' to have in your mind if you know that you need to speak briefly. You need only say a few sentences around these lines and know you have something strong to close on. Whoever advised J. K. Rowling in these circumstances did a good job. (Or maybe she advised herself.) The only thing I would change is her narrating her attempt to control her emotions. Although that is very sweet and enjoyable for the audience. What to do if you can't stop crying? Ideally keep going: don't berate yourself out loud for crying – we can see you're crying, we don't need to hear what's inside your head – just get on with it.

Interestingly, out of all the speeches in this book, it's this film-premiere one that is probably the closest to the sort of speech most women may be able to give in their everyday lives. Certainly they won't be giving it in Trafalgar Square in front of several thousand people and it won't be about a multi-million-pound film franchise that is the culmination of their entire career. And they almost certainly won't be as emotional as J. K. Rowling. But the structure is something to think about. It's four minutes and – if you take out the ad libs and the exclamations of 'Oh, my God' and 'Coherent . . .' (she is exhorting herself aloud to be coherent) – twenty-seven sentences long. I think almost anyone can write a twenty-seven-sentence speech of thanks. I also think it would be a lot better if it were only ten sentences long, if you're not J. K. Rowling and you don't need to deal with thousands of people chanting your name as you try to speak.

If anybody knows about audience expectation, it's probably J. K. Rowling, who has had to learn the art of timing across many thousands of words of storytelling. There's a moment in her Harvard speech when she feels the need to keep us posted on where she's up to: 'I'm nearly finished,' she says. Again, this is a sweet touch. It's not something that a more accomplished or arrogant speaker would say. It's as much for herself ('Thank God, I'm nearly finished') as it is for us (as if anyone would be wishing that J. K. Rowling would hurry up and finish) – and it's an excellent tip to remember. She gets herself through that experience by keeping it simple: start a story, weave it in with another story, reassure the audience (and yourself) that it will be over soon, finish on a strong and memorable quote from Plutarch: 'What we achieve inwardly will change our outer reality.'

That mention of 'outer reality' reminds me of one final thing. There's a major gaffe in the premiere speech that could have been easily avoided. She has a clutch bag. She has to hold the clutch bag and the microphone. This is a nightmare. Give someone the clutch bag to hold, love, next time, OK?

Tips and Tricks

— Not all of us will be invited to give a commencement speech in our lifetime, but the hallmarks of these speeches are useful in many different contexts. These speeches require you to tie together personal experience and universal wisdom, good themes to consider for any speaking opportunity: what's the most important life lesson you've learned? What's the best (and worst) advice you received growing up? What have you learned from failure? What did you wish you knew at the age of twenty-one (or sixteen or thirty . . .) that you know now?

— One of the reasons commencement speeches work so well is that they come imbued with a sense of occasion. Wherever you can bring this quality into a speech, it's worth it. What does this moment represent for you and for the audience? What is the shared experience? In the case of the commencement speech the subtext is: 'You're starting on a journey as a young person with the rest of your life ahead of you. I've also been in your shoes.' It's hard to see how that transfers to your sales conference but it can be done. What challenges do you share in common with the audience? What are the feelings you're having that they will be having too? What information, knowledge or experience do you have that will help them?

— We can't all be J. K. Rowling and be worshipped the second we appear on stage, not needing to say anything to be loved until our dying day. However, we can learn from her example: it's OK to hate speaking; it's OK to admit that in your speech; it's OK to make mistakes, mess up, cry and narrate your failure during the speech (but not too much, please). I wish we could see more speakers like her, instead of focusing on those able to set the bar so high at the Golden Globes or the Democratic Convention.

— Remember the clutch bag. Give yours to someone else to hold. Put your award down. Don't be fumbling with things while you're speaking. And while I'm on this subject, if you're ever giving a vote of thanks at an event where people are drinking, remember that they cannot applaud without putting their glasses down. So make sure you finish with a toast ('So, let's all raise a glass to . . .'), not with a request for applause. (This is really important to remember or you will end up thinking your speech was rubbish as you get a piddly smattering of clapping that is the inevitable result of over-occupied hands.)

Exercises

— Using the example of J. K. Rowling's twenty-seven-sentence thank-you speech, give yourself the task of writing three thank-you speeches for the same event. One should be three sentences long. The next can be seven sentences and the last thirteen. Read them out loud and time them. At what length do you feel most comfortable speaking? Can you imagine learning one of these versions, then ad-libbing around it? Can you use this exercise to suggest that you give a thank-you speech at a real event?

— Using the example of J. K. Rowling's seeming lack of preparation for her speech at the premiere (apart from one or two killer lines and memorizing the people she needed to thank), challenge yourself to give a short speech at an event where you weren't planning to speak. You'd be amazed at how easy it is to find these moments. Propose a toast at a party. Say thank you to the organizers at an event. Lead a 'three cheers' moment at a fundraiser. Promise yourself that you will do this, force yourself to go through with it and award yourself some kind of congratulations present when you've done it. Try to get someone to video it, then watch it back and (a) be really proud of yourself or (b) work out how you could do it better next time. (Ideally both.)

8

Be More Chimamanda: Chimichanga, Quiet Passion and How to Bring a Written Speech to Life

It's OK to speak from notes

Chimamanda Ngozi Adichie's two most legendary speeches have gone viral and had over 15 million views each. She has also given dozens of other speeches worth watching, including a recent one in which she talked about the importance of intention and what happened when she was introduced as 'Chimichanga'. Her conclusion: it's fine to call her Chimichanga by accident and if you tried hard to pronounce her name. It's not fine if you say it because you're too lazy to bother or you're mocking her. She did add that these things are not that big a deal for her as in her native language, Igbo, her name means: 'My personal spirit will not be broken.' I would suggest that you do not mess with such a person, not even accidentally.

Adichie's highly successful speeches are worth studying because she gives them on her own terms. She is not an improviser; she is not an emotional person; she is highly organized. I don't want to go too far into the realms of speculation but I would suggest from her stance and habits at these speeches – and from some of the insights into her character that she gives in them – she is probably a control freak. Many women can identify with that. Why leave an important speech to chance? Or to an autocue that might malfunction?

So, unlike many other TED Talkers, she reads from a lectern instead of pacing the stage. This gives us something to think about when we consider what it means to 'own the room'. You connect with the audience through your energy and excitement and by moving around. Or you can do it by standing your ground. Many speakers will say that you can't 'connect' in a meaningful way by reading something prepared that's in front of you. You need to learn it (and not use notes), you need an autocue or you need to be prepared to improvise. (I think elements of Ellen DeGeneres's commencement speech must have been improvised. She's an example of the opposite of a control freak.) But Chimamanda Ngozi Adichie's speech shows you can read aloud (about storytelling and feminism) and still have your words connect with an audience in an incredibly powerful way.

In her talk 'The Danger of a Single Story' she starts humbly and quietly. 'I'm a storyteller . . .' Her speech is serious and, initially, she does not actively seek to get laughs, even though she visibly relaxes – and is surprised – when they come. As well as standing behind a podium relying on her notes, she breaks a lot of other supposed rules of speaking early on: her physical stance is fidgety and wobbly, her eye contact is not consistent, she rushes slightly. She is clearly nervous and takes a few sentences to relax into her story. And yet. This talk has had over 15 million views and has had enormous impact.

This is another lesson in not needing to be perfect. For despite all these 'mistakes', her manner is completely compelling because we can tell that what she has to say matters to her. It feels as if she is taking a risk with what she's saying and yet she is completely confident precisely because it matters so much. She is also very good at signposting her ideas and clearly spelling them out to us – again, this is the skill of the professional writer: 'So what this did for me is this . . .' she will explain, providing absolute clarity. At the end she says, 'I would like to end with this thought . . .' There is not going to be an awkward moment when people think, Is that it? She is telling us the end is coming. You don't have to do this in a speech. But if you are a control freak, it will probably give you a lot of pleasure to do so. Everyone will know where they are.

She takes her time to pause between points and is not put off if she comes to the end of a point and has to look down at her paper to see where she's going next. This is a real skill and one worth practising. It's fine to take pauses at the end of thoughts or messages. In fact, it's necessary for the audience. They are not waiting to hear what you will say next. They are taking on board what you have just said. It's fine to give them time to do that, while you calmly look down and see what's coming next. Adichie demonstrates extreme comfort with her written text. She's not bothered that she's using it. She doesn't care what you think about the fact that she's using it. And she is going at her own pace.

Calm authority is the real hallmark of her speaking. Chimamanda Ngozi Adichie doesn't seek to impress, she seeks to explain and make her points clear. Nothing is flashy or showy. There is humility to her, even though she is presenting huge ideas about difference, otherness and prejudice. She wears her ideas lightly and brings them in a spirit of openness, not seeking to push them but instead laying them out gently and patiently. She is a model of great self-esteem, right down to letting us see that she is not 100 per cent relaxed about giving this speech. The experience is humbling to her. To be able to show the real confidence that comes with honesty and let your humility shine through is a true attribute.

You don't have to let off fireworks to wow a crowd

By the time Adichie comes to present her second TED Talk, 'We Should All Be Feminists', she has blossomed as a speaker. The first talk was superb. The number of views is proof of that. But with the second, you can see that she is there to enjoy the moment. She's on a bigger stage and she 'owns' it immediately, making much more eye contact with the audience than during her previous talk, which had more of the feel of a lecture. This second outing feels more personal and assured. Once again, she is reading from a lectern and has her text to fall back on. But with this performance, it feels as if she doesn't need it.

I love this speech because she enjoys it so much and she smiles so frequently. She intersperses ideas with personal anecdotes and takes such pure joy in saying, 'Now here's a story from my childhood . . .' as she leads us gently through moments of reminiscence that reveal something about the theory she wants to tease out. (Summary: it's a good idea to be a feminist.) Adichie succeeds in moving beyond the mentality of 'I am giving a speech.' She makes us forget that she is giving a speech. It feels as if she is talking intimately to us, face to face. Despite the veneer of formality and the cast-iron control she clearly has over the process, that is all stripped away in what feels like a one-to-one conversation.

This is the real knack of great speaking. You have to want to say it. You have to believe you have something worth sharing. You have to be excited about sharing it with other people. There are two sides to this. On the one hand, cultivating these feelings will help you to develop what you want to say, overcome your nerves and remember that it's not about you, it's about the audience. On the other, these feelings are a great way to guide yourself to *finding* something to talk about that really does fire you up. If you could set aside all your nerves, anxiety and reservations about speaking, what is the one thing you would love to share with people, the one thing that makes you feel excited just thinking about it? Let go of the idea that some people might not understand you, that it might be difficult, that some people might reject it. Imagine that the speech flies. Imagine that it soars. Imagine people love it. What would you say if that were the case? With every sentence of Adichie's feminism talk, it feels as if this is what she has said to herself beforehand: 'Delight them. That's all you need to do. Delight them. Explain. But do it joyfully.'

She's enjoying herself so much in this speech that when the audience laughs hard at particular points, she goes off script and ad libs, acknowledging that they've obviously experienced some of the things she has. (Going to a restaurant in Nigeria, for example, with a man and the waiter only acknowledging the man.) Yet despite how relaxed she is, she never deviates from the brilliant stillness she has in her posture. She has full control over the room, patrolling the entire audience with a gentle gaze. She holds her hands steadily, linked, in front of her, breaking that only occasionally to turn her pages. She does not lean into the audience or into the podium. She allows her body weight to fall back on to her heels so that we are drawn to her. She goes with whatever emotions come up during this twenty-minute talk. If she gets carried away laughing, she lets herself laugh.

But she's also not afraid of hand-brake turns in emotion. She moves from jokes and sarcasm to a friend who died in a plane crash. She keeps the audience on their toes, almost as if she's trying to keep herself on hers. There's a sense that she's challenging herself at the same time as challenging us.

We all make the mistake of watching a speaker like her and feeling so blown away that we don't examine what she's doing that works so well. It's partly because the content of her speech is so important and so beautifully written that we're completely distracted by it (and rightly so). In terms of learning how to speak, though, and drawing inspiration for ourselves from her performance, it helps to switch off from the meaning of the speech and just look at how she inhabits it. We're predisposed to enjoy the content because she teaches us to do so by how she is standing and holding herself. Of course, the way you genuinely feel can't be faked and the proof of this is the difference between the first speech ('The Danger of a Single Story') and the second ('We Should All Be Feminists'). There were three years between the two speeches and in between something in Adichie has changed: she is fully willing to accept how good she is, how ready the world is to hear her and how easy this is for her.

Let it be easy

One of the reasons it is worth watching and re-watching Chimamanda Ngozi Adichie many times is her ease. She inhabits herself and her ideas in a relaxed and easygoing way, as if to say, 'Take it or leave it. But I think you might find this interesting. I don't mind, though, if you don't.' This is an incredibly rare quality. Instead I constantly see an unwillingness towards the concept of 'ease' in accomplished women.

They are extremely resistant to the idea that anything might be easy or uncomplicated. They are not keen to relax or to enjoy their speech. They want it to be difficult because they have bought the myth that it has to be difficult. Meanwhile, at work events, they will have watched male colleagues, unprepared and unstressed, bluffing and getting away with it. I'm not saying all men do this but some men do. And it's extremely rare to see a woman do it. Why not be the woman who tries it sometime? Why not be the one who coasts? Why not be the one who says afterwards, 'I didn't even really prepare for that and I found it easy'?

Of course, the real reason Adichie can be so free and easy in herself is because she has prepared meticulously for years beforehand. She has put in the ground work as a writer and a thinker. But this is true for all of us as long as we're talking about the right subject. We all have something we're expert on that others would like to know about. We have all mastered things that others find difficult to master.

What's striking about Adichie's content is that, although it is intelligent, smart, of a very high quality and almost academic, it always remains accessible. Her speeches pass quickly and easily for the audience and we don't feel as though we've sat through a lecture, rather that we've learned something and have somehow been improved by her words – effortlessly. This is a wonderful feeling to give an audience.

How does she do it? She mixes personal stories – which she emphasizes, using a conspiratorial and intimate tone – and theory. She has a number of key points she wants to make about, say, prejudice, creativity, gender, culture, but she does not overload us with facts or ideas. Instead, she intersperses her speeches with stories: 'Let me tell you about a good friend of mine'; 'I have a very dear friend . . .'; 'There was a time in my childhood . . .'; 'When I was last on a night out in Lagos . . .'. What works brilliantly about these stories is that they are simple, not burdened with detail and believable. We don't think for a minute that she's introducing them as a rhetorical device. They feel like real moments from her life that she's sharing with us. They make you wish she was your friend. Or even half believe that she is.

This is a great trick for any speech, especially one you're struggling with. Think of something that connects you personally to the idea. A conversation you once had, a person you knew, an encounter, an observation. And find a way to link it into the ideas in your speech. I know this sounds hard if you're giving a work speech about something like marketing or branding, but there must be something about it that you find entertaining or an idea in the presentation that reminds you of something a friend once said that amused you or a quote you've never forgotten. If you're truly stumped and you can't find anything personal to connect you to a speech, then I would say – fairly harshly – that you may well be in the wrong job. There is no way that, long term, any of us can give presentations we find boring and have no personal meaning to us. Struggling to find personal meaning in a speech is a red flag. It's the very opposite of what is going on in a Chimamanda Ngozi Adichie speech where she is explaining the motivation that guides her as a writer and as a human being.

Finding the personal in something is key to so many things. First, it keeps you interested while you're preparing it. In 'We Should All Be Feminists', Adichie clearly wants to honour the memory of her friend who died in the plane crash, even though he is mentioned only very briefly and she doesn't make the whole speech about him. Nonetheless, his memory is clearly a motivator. Second, it gives the audience something emotional to latch on to, which they will remember even if they don't remember anything else. Once we hear a speaker talking about their personal experience or telling us something conversational we relax. We are not at school. This is not a lecture. We are not going to be tested. The speaker is happy to carry us and make it easy for us. You might need to get creative to find out what the equivalents are for you, but we all have them.

Show us what we have in common with you

A later speech by Adichie was even more confident. If you check out the opening of her Harvard Commencement speech of 2018, it's ridiculously brazen in its simplicity. She begins with a brief 'Hello' and 'Thank you' and gets a round of applause just for that. It's worth watching for her phrasing and how she allows the joy of what she's saying to show in her face. She looks truly honoured, humbled and grateful to be there, and that is what the audience responds to. She barely needs to say anything to open because her status means she doesn't need to.

This is a speech about truth and lies, in our writing, in our speech, and how that relates to politics. Adichie's simplicity is what makes the political content more palatable. She talks about the times she has lied: about her height, about being stuck in traffic when she is really still at home getting ready. She doesn't make herself find outlandish or complicated examples. She is not afraid of the mundane. Of course, you can get away with this if you're Chimamanda Ngozi Adichie. Her bearing is regal and commands respect. Anything she says that suggests she is a normal human being who is late for lunch with her friends because she can't decide what to wear, well, it makes her seem more approachable. She's a great lesson in finding ways to connect with the audience by showing that parts of your life are just like theirs.

Adichie goes on to talk about developing a 'bullshit detector' not only for others but for ourselves. This is so true for speaking. When we're preparing to say something, whether it's off the cuff or prepared, are we saying what we really want to say? Or are we bullshitting? Is there any way you can put something into your words that is emphatically not bullshit? Can you dare to say something that is real and bold? Of course, this is another reason why speeches by great speakers are sometimes not the ideal model for our own speaking because in the real world we have to contend with bosses, colleagues, rivals, the human-resources department. In real-life work situations, your speech may be vetted by others or even written by them and there may be little you can do about it. You may have to accept compromises or include some boring bits because the corporate communications department insists on it. Chimamanda Ngozi Adichie does not have to put up with that kind of interference. She is free to say whatever she chooses.

Anyone would be inspired by Adichie, but remember that if she had to give a speech about next year's project investment yield without being able to say what she really thought was likely – but instead what her boss wanted her to say – well, that would probably be as dull as it sounds. (I don't know what an investment yield is, by the way. Just in case that wasn't already clear.) Let her example challenge us all to reach higher than what is in front of us: find something true, find something meaningful. Yes, we can't all reach the standard of a Nobel Prize-winning novelist in our speaking. But we can find one true thing to say that means something to us. And we can find the thing that connects us to those we're speaking to.

Tips and Tricks

— Be honest with yourself about whether you are the sort of person who feels more confident if you are meticulously rehearsed or whether you work better when you can improvise and come up with things at the last minute. Sometimes it's good to put ourselves in situations where we can experiment with both disciplines. Obviously this isn't easy to do in a work context if you feel you could be sacked for being under-prepared for a presentation. But try to seek out situations in which it's safe to find ease through improvisation, even being slightly under-prepared and ready for anything. Pinpoint other situations that may benefit from a carefully rehearsed, pre-written speech, which you learn to deliver in an off-the-cuff way. There's a lot of joy and freedom to be found in moving between the two styles, as you can see when you look at Chimamanda Ngozi Adichie's different speeches.

— Remind yourself that one of the main reasons to take on speaking challenges is to increase your experience of leadership (if this is what matters to you). Leaders are not in control of everything. Sometimes they don't know if they're going to have to give a speech. They may be called upon to do so when they're not in control of all the facts. They may have to step in for someone else who has dropped out and improvise the entire thing without anyone in the audience ever guessing. This is real leadership. In workshops, when I present women with these scenarios, they are horrified. They want a guarantee that they can prepare, have all the facts at their fingertips and be sure that they will not make a mistake. This is not real life. And this is not real leadership. Putting yourself in low-pressure situations where you can rehearse improvisation and making-it-up-as-you-go-along is the only thing that will prepare you for real leadership. Don't wait until you're ready. Do it when you're not ready.

Exercises

— Find a text you can read aloud. It could be the opening page of a book, a speech you've given or a speech you've found on the internet. (There are transcripts of many of the speeches in this book online. I love to see how many words the speech was and how many minutes that translated into; how many points were covered; how many laughs; how many applause moments . . . I'm a sad person. But this is incredibly useful for preparing your own speeches. These things are a template, a dream template.) So, find a speech. Practise standing as if you're at a podium and read it aloud, while trying to deliver it as if you're not reading it. You might have to read through it a few times before you can do this. Practise reading a line in your head, then saying it out loud to the audience (without looking down). Practise taking long pauses. See what it feels like to try to deliver this text when it's in front of you and you haven't learned it, but you're 'reading' it without simply reading it. What I'm trying to get you to do is the opposite of what a school child does when they bring a text right up to their face and read each word individually without imbuing any sense or meaning.

— Get ready to record yourself on your phone. Think of a topic to speak on, whether it's something you know a little about, a pet theme or a vote of thanks at an event. Don't make it imaginary. Make it real. Set yourself the challenge of speaking for one minute or for ten sentences (count them on your fingers) completely improvised, while you record yourself. Now try it two more times with two different subjects. Listen back. Don't be overly critical. What did you do well? Could you have got away with it in front of people? Might you be better scripted? Or did you surprise yourself? Make it easier by deciding what your last sentence (or thought) will be before you start speaking.

9

Be More Angela: Stillness, Temple Fingers and Gravitas (with Help from Hillary Clinton, Christine Lagarde, Gloria Steinem)

Holding back can be just as powerful as holding forth

Perhaps one of the most surprising things about political speakers and campaigners is that their speeches are often very restrained. When Angela Merkel and Emmanuel Macron launched the Élysée Treaty in 2018 ('The EU's road map to reforms'), they released a video of the two of them explaining what the treaty is. It's exciting, guys! (It's not. But it is short and quite funny.) It's a short address where their two styles – charismatic French versus homely German – emerge as markedly different. Macron's body language, expression and tone say, 'Please like me.' It's not unpleasant. He is happy high status and has tons of attractive presence. Merkel comes across as the more forceful one. She keeps completely still – in terms of her eye contact, posture and head movements – and holds her hands in front of her in the 'temple' position. (Fingertips touching. Think Mr Burns in *The Simpsons*.) The only time she moves is when she uses the word 'strong' and then she makes a fist with her hand. This is a really great illustration of two very different kinds of leadership, each effective in its own way. But what Merkel projects most of all is a studied, trustworthy neutrality.

Incidentally it can be difficult in situations where you're sharing a stage to know how to stand when the other person is talking. Do you look at them, nod and smile? Or do you look, with no expression, at the audience? It's interesting to watch TV duos when they have to do this. It's a real art to seem engaged but not too engaged (otherwise you look demented), to appear neutral but not bored. Merkel looks out neutrally but she is also relaxed and very close to happy high status. But not too happy. She's not that kind of person. She adopts another neutral hand position, too, clasping her hands in front of her. (Less threatening than the 'temple' position. She loves the temple position. She's doing it in the photograph on her Wikipedia page and in virtually every other official photograph of her.)

I am slightly obsessed with power-sharing on stage and what you should do when you're visible but not talking. This is also something useful to think about in case you're facilitating or on a panel. You need to perfect your 'listening' face and posture. I always advise having a pen because it gives you something to do with your hands. You look engaged but not distracting. The same goes for when you need to share a stage with someone. It probably wouldn't be appropriate for Angela Merkel to hold a pen in this particular situation. In fact, it would be weird. Instead, she stands firm. It's very amusing at the end when she has to speak in French (which she is clearly uncomfortable with) and smile. She really doesn't want to do either.

There's something human, real and warming about her dis-comfort. She is clearly happier issuing instructions and showing leadership. Macron is much more comfortable with movement, dynamism and levity. Each to their own.

The power of doing as little with your body as possible

Now, I know I have gone on about stillness quite a lot. But Angela Merkel shows that it really matters in the projection of leadership. The speaking hallmark of veteran politicians, like her and Hillary Clinton, is stillness. They will make a point of barely moving at all while giving a speech. Hold-ing your ground and silently commanding a room creates a powerful impression before you have spoken a word. Just as Angela Merkel always wears the same suit but in different colours (so that no one can ever comment on what she is wearing), she has clearly adopted a similar atti-tude towards her public-speaking technique: discipline, calm, focus.

Hillary is similar, although she has been able to relax a little since she's no longer seeking office. She, too, uses the Mr Burns 'temple' fingertips-touching hand position a lot, and I wonder if with both women this is to achieve still-ness. It stops you fidgeting and keeps your hands visible when it can look odd to put them behind your back. 'Tem-ple' hand position makes you look as if you're thinking about an important strategic decision. I must admit that I never use it on stage or anywhere else, perhaps because I'm never thinking about an important strategic decision. And also because I don't want to look like Mr Burns.

Women who can borrow these tactics and stay almost creepily still during speaking notice that people pay much closer attention to what they're saying. Easy to learn. Difficult to do. Great results. Merkel is a good person to study, especially if you're not a German speaker. Anyone who projects authority, confidence and leadership in a language you don't know is a useful person to observe because you aren't distracted by the words: you can focus purely on the way they put things across.

Everything about her is somehow appropriate. She speaks with simplicity, clarity and restrained warmth. She does not attempt jokes or friendliness. She is happy to go for the absolute average in all things. There is nothing noticeable about her, nothing over-the-top. This is very much the Merkel way. It is low-risk, safe and comfortable. In more improvised settings, such as TV debates with opponents, she follows the same style but loosens it slightly: she holds on to the podium, using one hand to gesture but with extreme discipline. In her annual address to the German people on New Year's Eve, her posture is always almost supernaturally calm (but not in a disturbing way). She always likes to hold her hands together in front of her or resting on something, such as a podium or a desk.

She is not about showing passion. She is about showing quiet, controlled strength. She represents predictability and security.

Political Leadership Style 1: Captain Sensible

I can feel you saying, 'But I don't want to be like Angela Merkel. I want to be like Michelle Obama.' Yes, I know, we all do. But the point is, Angela Merkel could never be Michelle Obama, even if she wanted to. And I'm sure she doesn't. She's very much herself. Finding a personal style that suits her has been her great strength. She has held Germany's highest office since 2005. Clearly people respond positively to her leadership style and she has seen off many challenges. It's very important that we respect her staid, calm, quiet style and learn from it. Perhaps more women would go into politics if they knew they could behave like this and didn't have to give fire-and-brimstone speeches that make you want to cry. Merkel does things by the book. She's sensible. She follows the headmistress path. It might not be modern or exciting but it suits her, and her track record is proof that it works. Merkel is one of the most valuable examples we have of a female leader who has found a style that suits her personality and her environment. I don't suggest that people should copy her. But I do think it would be amazing if every woman could find a personal leadership style as suited to her as Merkel's is to her.

Her speaking has been described as 'a masterclass in detachment', which is both a great compliment and an insult. It's a compliment in that she is able to approach very difficult topics (immigration, terrorism) with dispassion and a clear head. She explains the nuances and difficulties of her position with ultimate calm. But it's also an insult as she is rarely able to bring passion into her defence of her decisions, which can make her seem cold. Yet this has clearly been the right tone for the times, as her record shows.

This approach did not lead in the same direction for Hillary Clinton. Let's remind ourselves that she attracted more votes than Donald Trump without actually winning the presidency. But in 2016 her style, which is similar to Angela Merkel's – old-school, calm, sensible, don't-rock-the-boat – was ultimately not a winning formula. In theory Hillary Clinton is another master of controlled, quiet power. In reality there was something about her manner that didn't sit right with the electorate. Or perhaps something about her manner didn't fit her properly. It's easy to suggest that this didn't work out for her because she 'lost the presidency'. But there's another way to think of it, which is to focus on her successes.

Her manner and talents gave her a four-decade career in politics, culminating in a four-year stint as secretary of state and a memorable presidential bid in which she won the biggest share of the vote. So while her style may not ultimately have been 'winning', something about it served her well.

Clinton's speaking is measured and follows the same 'headmistress' qualities of Merkel. This is certainly a generational thing: there are sixteen years between Hillary Clinton and Michelle Obama. And it's always worth remembering that Michelle Obama has never run for or held political office. By contrast, Hillary – perhaps unlike her opponent for the presidency – takes political office extremely seriously and never once let her guard down when she was in pursuit of it.

Ironically, since she has stepped away from that world, her speaking has been praised as more 'authentic'. But she would argue that you can't win – people want to criticize you as a woman, no matter what you do. I'm not entirely convinced that Hillary Clinton was ever really free to find the leadership style that worked for her as her career was so dogged by controversies, many of them relating to her husband. She herself argued that she was over-scrutinized because she was a woman. In *Dear Madam President*, her communications director, Jennifer Palmieri, mentions passing on comments advising her on her speaking style. Her response was always along these lines: 'If they could just let us know which woman has the perfect speaking style?' There was never any answer to this question.

Political Leadership Style 2: Elder Stateswoman

Like Merkel's, Clinton's style is characterized by a discreet show of power: very few smiles, very little emotion, just a hint of warmth. In her speech at the 2016 Democratic Convention when she accepted the nomination for the presidency, she received gigantic applause while standing calmly, holding her hands together. The cheering goes on for much longer than she wants it to and she tries to silence the audience by repeatedly saying, 'Thank you.' (She doesn't hold her hands up, which would probably have achieved it quicker.) She forces her voice more than she needs to. This is something stadium speakers often forget, I think: the crowd may not be able to hear everything but the speaker is amplified by a microphone so doesn't need to raise her voice. She speaks slowly, deliberately, aiming her gaze around the room. The voice is much more forceful than, say, Michelle Obama's: it is the voice of someone who is seeking office. Michelle Obama can afford to be more intimate. She doesn't need to get anyone to vote for her.

Clinton's great strength is that she has been doing this for forty years so she has an endless supply of ideas, quotes and tricks she can draw on in a speech. Her style is effortless and familiar. She is very good at punctuating her points with her hand movements, which she is careful not to overuse. She makes good use of her qualities as a traditional speaker, quoting Franklin D. Roosevelt and leading the crowd as she chants, 'The only thing we have to fear is fear itself.' In the first moments of the speech she refers to the fact that she met her husband 'in the law library' forty-five years ago: a great way to bring in a hint of personal intimacy without saying anything cheesy or revealing. But it's also a great way of reminding the audience that she trained as a lawyer. (She was the first female partner in the law firm where she worked in the late 1970s.)

The biggest lesson to draw from Hillary is to feel comfortable with your own wisdom and experience and not be afraid to let it show. Let others take it or leave it. It's not as if you can pretend you're something you're not. She has been training as a persuasive and controlled speaker since she was a teenager. Nothing is going to trip her up – apart from people's constant scrutiny of her as a woman and the fact that she never seemed to measure up to some mythical ideal. In *Dear Madam President*, Jennifer Palmieri says that, since the 1970s, when the public were asked what they thought of Hillary Clinton, they would always reply, 'There's just something about her . . .' with the unfinished implication '. . . that I don't like.' Palmieri sees this as being about the American people's inherent resistance to being governed by a woman – or even to the idea of an ambitious woman seeking power. She hopes it will change in the years to come.

Political Leadership Style 3: Sensible, Sassy, Wise Woman

Christine Lagarde may not be someone whose speeches have had international impact in the way Michelle Obama's have. But she is definitely someone whose style is useful for aspiring female leaders to examine. She speaks in a relaxed, conversational way. When she gives speeches in English it's not her first language so she's careful to speak slowly to make her meaning clear. Remember that if you're a native speaker there may always be someone in your audience who doesn't speak English fluently: keep them in mind and slow down.

And do think about the task Christine Lagarde, Angela Merkel or even Melania Trump face: when they speak to a global audience they are often not using their first language. In Christine Lagarde's lengthy speeches on economics, she speaks with an awareness that she is being simultaneously translated, so she needs to leave time and space for that. As she gets further into a speech, she speeds up, having let the audience get used to her voice. She usually works from notes but often appeals directly to the audience with ad libs and questions. She is far more seductive and persuasive than Hillary Clinton or Angela Merkel. She almost always opens her speeches with a broad smile.

Lagarde's job is politically sensitive and involves her

having to be something of a diplomat. She is often impart-ing information or putting across a theory, rather than setting out an argument or sharing a passion. She uses her hands sparingly but, when she does, her signature gestures are expansive. In a public address to Harvard Kennedy School's Institute of Politics, she describes the world economy through the metaphor of weather and uses her hands to illustrate sunshine, rain clouds, a storm. It keeps our interest going in a speech that is otherwise serious and heavy-going. (She often uses this weather metaphor in her appearances, with a JFK quote in reference to the economy: 'The time to repair the roof is when the sun is shining.')

One of the things I find most amusing about Lagarde's speaking is that she never varies her tone. Yes, she settles into a speech and speeds up a tiny bit. But apart from that she maintains an even tone so religiously that you think she's got a metronome underneath the podium. There is an extraordinary precision to her speaking and she is very easy to understand, even though she is usually talking about complicated fiscal policies and using economic jargon. She is a model of calm and predictability, a safe pair of hands. She differs slightly from Merkel and Clinton in that she projects knowledge, wisdom and insight rather than authority, power and political leader-ship, although these things are frequently intertwined. She's a useful role model for anyone working for a conservative organization threatened by female power. She's also useful for women who don't find it easy to step into the spotlight: she owns it in a very respectable and sensible way.

Political Leadership Style 4: Maverick Campaigner

Campaigning speaker energy is very different from the kind of energy we see in elected politicians and in those seeking election. Campaigners have to argue their cause but in many ways they have nothing to prove: they know what they stand for and either you're on board or you're not. They can stick to their guns and be unambiguous in a way politicians often cannot.

What's striking about Gloria Steinem's 1970 speech at the USA Women's Liberation Rally is how nonchalant she is. This is not an angry woman screaming that the world must change. She's talking up close into a microphone on a podium in order to be heard and she's reading a script out loud. It is not a rallying cry. It's a statement that feels a bit like a health and safety warning. She actually sounds quite bored and as if she's just getting through it. There's a surprising quiet power at work here, as if she's saying: 'I believe these things and I don't want to get agitated to convince you that I'm right.' She only pauses and raises her tone on her last point: 'I will no longer accept society's judgement that my group is second class.' She looks up proudly and the applause begins.

The contrast with her appearance at the 2017 Women's March in Washington DC is striking: she's far more relaxed. Although Steinem still looks exactly the same she allows herself an ad lib and a broad smile – 'I wish you could see yourselves. It's like an ocean.' But she is still carrying a sheaf of papers, like last time, and is clearly only comfortable saying what she has come prepared to say. This time, however, she knows how to get the crowd's attention – she raises a hand, like a teacher, showing that she is about to start and they should settle. 'OK, I need to be short,' she says. She uses her hands a lot now, often drawing one to her chest to emphasize something she cares about deeply.

Steinem's speaking is another example of how low the bar is. Her speaking is not that special. What's special is that it's Gloria Steinem doing it and she's putting into words what others cannot. The content is more important than the delivery. With Steinem, it is not about the manner of her speaking. It is all about what she's saying and the fact that she's saying it at all. The lesson? We don't need to be afraid of the audience's response if we have important things to say, but we're not powerhouse speakers. Gloria Steinem is not a powerhouse speaker. And look at what she achieved.

The same goes for Emma Watson's 'He for She' 2014 speech at the United Nations, which has had over 7 million views on YouTube. She starts so slowly and deliberately!

Initially there is no smile or authority to her presence. There's a wobble in her voice because she's nervous and because she's emotional about her subject matter. This doesn't lessen the speech, though, it personalizes it. It reminds us that she is speaking not as a celebrity but as an ordinary human being. There's something very powerful and edgy about a speaker who is not quite in control of the material they're presenting. We're mesmerized because we don't know if they're going to break down or not. She lists all the things that led her to feminism: being told as an eight-year-old that she is bossy for wanting to direct plays; being sexualized in the media from the age of fourteen; seeing her friends drop out of school sports teams because they don't want to become 'too muscly'. Her voice wavers more and more, and it's not just nerves: you can tell how much all this means to her.

Emma Watson is a fascinating example. She's a trained actor and she could presumably 'act' the role of a more confident speaker if she wanted to. But she chooses to give this speech as herself, warts and all. It's the opposite of a performance: it's a true account of someone who finds the subject matter difficult and risky to talk about. She's also nervous because she's criticizing other women, effectively calling out anyone who doesn't want to identify as a feminist. You can feel her anxiety about their judgement as she speaks.

How does she keep going in this speech without

losing it, even though her voice seems about to break at any moment? Extreme stillness. Keeping her head almost as still as her body. Keeping her hands and arms in the same place, without them looking frozen or locked. This is a good technique: if you're nervous, focus on your stillness. She visibly relaxes five minutes in when she gets a round of applause from her audience who have felt how difficult it is for her to deliver this message. Once she relaxes, she allows herself to use her hands a bit more.

There's a moment when she makes a mistake, talking about the pressure on men to appear strong. She says that some men are afraid to express their emotions for fear of seeming 'less of a men'. She corrects herself to 'less of a man' without a beat and we know that she's OK with the mistake so we forget it instantly. This is the key to letting yourself become emotional in a speech (or giving yourself permission to be nervous): be present in the moment, listen to what is coming out of your mouth, and if you make a mistake, correct it, then move on calmly. Don't reference the mistake, don't beat yourself up, don't apologize. If you are nervous, you can reference it once you have established yourself firmly and not until halfway through the speech. As Emma Watson says: 'In my nervousness for this speech and in my moments of doubt, I've told myself firmly, if not me, who? If not now, when? If you have similar doubts when opportunities are presented to you, I hope those words will be helpful.'

Tips and Tricks

— If you're delivering something with difficult information (Emma Watson's reference to the male suicide rate, for example), decide whether you're going to be neutral or whether you'll show how this information affects you. She is clearly affected by it and lets her passion show. In order to be able to keep speaking while you feel emotional, remember to breathe between sentences, stay focused on your next point so that you don't lose your thread, and give the audience plenty of time to take in what you're saying.

— A campaigning speech does not have to be full of passion, fire and brimstone. It can be a sober listing of all the facts. Or it can be a low-key but intimate *cri de coeur* that lets the audience see clearly how you've been affected.

— For a great example of how to stand up in the middle of a charity gala with just a microphone, no stage, people in front of and behind you (so that you don't know where to look), check out Viola Davis's short speech at the 2017 Time 100 Gala. This is not a great speech as it's not entirely clear what she's talking about. She tells a long story about visiting a tribe in the Gambia where infertile women are supported by the rest of their community.

She then attempts to bring this round by noting the relevance to everyone in the room who has ever done something for someone else. Maybe you had to be there. The point is, she gets away with it because of the sincerity of the delivery, the measured tone of her voice and her poise in assuming that everyone will listen. She doesn't have to appeal to them, she can just reel them in by standing her ground (admittedly she has the advantage of being Viola Davis). This is a fine example of how you can get away with looking like you've given a great speech simply by looking as if you have. You don't actually have to give a great speech.

Exercises

— What are the things you care about on a grand scale? This may or may not have something to do with your work. The environment? Poverty? An illness that has affected your life or that of someone close to you? A political injustice? A local scandal? Make a list of five things that interest you or have captured your attention. Now choose three and write the title of a two-minute speech you could give on each topic about why you care.

— Under the title of each, write down three quotes (you can search online) or three sentences you could use in this speech. Make one something you could finish on.

— Get out your phone and record yourself giving one of these speeches, with your notes in front of you. Improvise for no more than two minutes, making sure you incorporate all three quotes or sentences and that you end on the line you identified to finish on. Listen back and note three things you did well and three things you could do differently.

10

Be More You: The Trouble
with Nerves, Reading
Your Speech Like
Mr Bean, and the
Women Drummers

Lesson: the only way to do it is to do it

The moment when everything changes for Katherine Graham (played by Meryl Streep) in *The Post* is a moment of sudden realization: 'Oh! That's it! I've had enough! I'm speaking up.' At this point in the film Graham is hesitating over an important decision that could make or break the newspaper – and could also result in her going to jail. She has to decide whether to publish from the Pentagon Papers. There are good arguments both for and against. A man tries to interrupt her to put across his opinion while she is trying to get her mind clear on a point. Suddenly, out of nowhere, she controls her exasperation, spins on her heels and says firmly and clearly: 'I'm talking to Mr Bradlee now.'

It's a small moment but it's the turning point of her life and her leadership. All it took was for her to step into the opportunity that was already there. No one could give it to her. She had to take it. It's time for us all to turn around and tell the world that they can all bloody well shut up because we're talking to Mr Bradlee now.

This book isn't a guide for women who feel physically

sick about public speaking and just want to survive the one horrific time they're asked to give a speech and can't say no because their boss will be annoyed – although I hope it will help those people. This is a book for those who want to speak or get better at it but feel a tiny bit sick and/or don't know where or how to start. It cannot take the anxiety away. But it does give you some tricks for living with it or lessening it. Exposure lessens it most, and the more frequent exposure the better. There is no other cure. And, let's be honest, not even frequent exposure cures it completely.

Perhaps a far scarier thing than the fear itself is the business of making the speaking happen. This is about women deciding to put themselves forward. You have to choose to make your own opportunities to speak. No one ever invited anyone to give a TED Talk. (Seriously, they didn't.) Those people applied. They went through a difficult selection process and sometimes an audition. Their topic and their speech? All unsolicited. They didn't just get a call out of the blue saying, 'We're looking for speakers and we love you. Talk about whatever you want.' This hardly ever happens in any industry or walk of life. You have to make yourself known. You have to make your own luck. You have to set up your own events. You have to nominate yourself as the speaker, as the chairperson, as the facilitator. As the careers guru Seth Godin puts it: 'Choose yourself.' Why? Because we no longer live in an era where you have to wait for a newspaper advert to appear with your dream job description in it. You can write your own. You can book yourself for your own speech.

The best way of going about this is to start to tell people that you want to speak. Meanwhile you can get some low-level practice in easy environments. I can already feel you saying, 'But what will I talk about?' Content is another subject, but it shouldn't over-burden us. As discussed, around 80 per cent of any communication is non-verbal. So, yes, of course you want good content, but it will be completely ruined unless you deliver it in a relaxed and engaging way.

One way to generate ideas for speaking is to ask the person you're dealing with, 'If I came to speak to your students, what would they want to know from me?' The answer is the title of your talk. 'If I come and talk to your department, what would they most want to hear? What would they least want to hear?' You can also ask friends. 'If I could teach you something I know a lot about, what would it be?' We all tend to take for granted our areas of expertise, which others envy. Make the effort to find out what these are. You may well have areas of expertise that bore you and you don't want to talk about. That's fine. Keep going until you hit one that does fire you up. (See more on this in A guide to creating speaking opportunities, p. 225.)

If you find yourself thinking, But I don't have anything interesting or important to say, I'm sorry, but this is utter bullshit. As Susan Cain says: 'The world needs you and it needs the things you carry.' Everyone has something interesting and important to say because they have their individual perspective. All you need to do is find the perspective that's appropriate for your audience. My seven-year-old could give a great speech to his school assembly about why he feels proud of England's performance in the 2018 World Cup. This wouldn't be such a great TED Talk. (Actually it might. He's pretty funny.) Similarly, you could give an entertaining and inspiring overview of your team's work performance at the end-of-year office party. This would not be appropriate at your child's school assembly.

The important thing to remember is that in real life the majority of speeches are not 'I Have a Dream' moments, designed to shift the fabric of the universe. They are off-the-cuff, unprepared remarks given by someone in a position of authority to impart information, say thank you or provide some kind of low-level inspiration to get us through another day at work. One of the tricks of great speaking is to accept it for what it is: not that different from an everyday conversation or interaction. You're just doing it in front of a larger group of people. We spend an awful lot of time worrying when we're asked to 'say a few words'. In reality this annoying little phrase spells out exactly what we are being asked to do: say a few words. That's it. Don't say too much. (Three or five sentences may be enough.) It doesn't have to be hilarious or heartwarming. Say your bit, keep it short, sit down. Job done.

Do whatever it takes to make it less intimidating for you

My final wish is for every woman to make it easy on herself. This may sound crazy coming at the end of an entire book with hundreds of different pieces of advice on public speaking, but the best advice of all is to take the effort out of it, relax and have fun. Do whatever is in your power to find something to enjoy about your presentation or invent something about it that makes you laugh or smile. I don't mean that you have to make the audience laugh (although this helps in almost any circumstance) but that you have to find something during your preparation that makes you laugh, whether it's laughing at yourself and how stressed you are, or laughing at a stupid subtitle you have discarded ('My Half-arsed, Over-ambitious, Insane Conclusion') or making yourself laugh by reading the whole thing in a Mr Bean voice for practice.

We take ourselves way too seriously and we take our speaking way too seriously. The audience is not interested in all that. They want to see you at your most relaxed. So lighten up. There are so many important and terrible things in the world. Your public-speaking moment, work presentation or stand-up set is not one of those things. So wear it lightly and let yourself enjoy it. I say this from bitter experience, having gone through several years of making my own performance very difficult for myself because I bought the myth that it should be hard work.

When I think of Mindy Tucker's photographs of the comedians in New York, I have to ask what I would to say to my former self, almost ten years on from starting stand-up comedy. And this is it: 'It's hard for everyone. That doesn't mean it has to be especially hard for you. Yes, it's hard work but that can be enjoyable. Draw strength from the moments when you love it. Be ready for it to be surprisingly easy sometimes and don't second-guess yourself. Don't listen to other people too much. Trust your own instincts. Get better. And I know you won't do this because it will seem too much like hassle but go and see a voice coach and train your voice every day. But most of all: don't sweat it so badly.'

My wish for any woman reading this book is that they drop the idea that they have some kind of problem. You know that saying: 'You know what her problem is?' Well, what if she doesn't have a problem? What if there's really nothing wrong with her speaking? She just needs to let herself speak. In my experience, this is exactly what is going on with a lot of women. Their natural instinct is good. Their natural communication skills are good. They can present competently and engagingly. Their problem is not their speaking. It is themselves. They question their excellence. They question their instincts. They wonder whether it's OK to enjoy it. They won't let it be easy. They shy away from the question: 'What if I don't have a problem?'

What if you don't? What would you say then? What

talk would you give? What if the reality is that you should have been speaking for years already, and now you've got to make up for lost time?

The nerves are never going away

The fear of speaking is entirely normal and is not going to disappear, no matter how much you speak. Think of all the great performers who have talked about their nerves: Ella Fitzgerald, Luciano Pavarotti, Stephen Fry, Daniel Day-Lewis, Laurence Olivier, Mikhail Baryshnikov (who has said that, no matter how rarely or often he performs, the stage fright 'never doesn't come'). Adele is said to vomit before she goes on stage. Barbra Streisand performs live only for charity because of her nerves. Carly Simon took six years off from live performance and has said she would rather play the tambourine than be the lead singer. Bette Midler has talked about lifelong performance anxiety and how she is plagued with the thoughts: Will people like you? Will they ask you back? Did I make the cut?

Some of these people learned to tolerate their nerves and work with them. Others changed their career path. The point is, nerves have nothing to do with talent or ability. They merely indicate that your central nervous system is working. What you do with that information, and how you cope with it, is up to you.

When I find myself getting nervous about a speaking

moment or a performance, I ask myself the following questions: Is this happening because I am under-prepared? If so, what can I do to over-prepare? (Note: I think of it as something that is happening to me. Not something that I *am*.) Is it because I'm tired, hungry, thirsty, anxious about other things? If so, I should deal with those things. Is it because I'm worried about the audience's reaction? If so, how can I work out what they may be feeling and going through? This is key for a lot of people: remembering that it isn't all about you. Just thinking about what other people at the event may be going through privately can be enough to shake you out of the self-obsession that comes with nerves.

I'll always remember one Edinburgh show I did where early on I spoke to someone in the audience. The person I picked out had a chronic (truly chronic) speech impediment. It was an excruciating moment for everyone in the room and immediately humbling for me. In a single second I saw how selfish it is to be nervous and care what everyone thinks of you, the person on stage. I can remember thinking: Why are you so focused on yourself? You think other people don't have things to contend with? You should be ashamed.

In some ways, our nerves are a form of narcissism. We think that everyone will be looking at us, judging us, evaluating us, caring about us. In reality we're nothing to other people (in a good way) and most people are focused on the worries and cares they have in their own lives. If the problem you have in life is that you're a bit nervous about your speaking, well, that is a bloody good problem to have. I realize that sounds harsh, but I know that this real-ization has been a life-changing epiphany for a lot of people I've worked with. The more experience you have in front of an audience, the more you realize that it's not about you. It's incredibly freeing to grasp that. It actually lets you off the hook.

Be happy high status wherever you are

One last word on why happy high status is sometimes eas-ier for men than women. Every piece of research shows that as a species we're more liable to award status to men than to women. This happens on and off the page. If you show a group of people CVs with women's names versus CVs with men's, people will usually choose the men over the women as leaders. In a group where no one has spoken, most people will choose a man as the natural leader. These biases are real because of years of social and cultural con-ditioning. They will take time to change. Similarly, women do not have as much opportunity to practise high status compared to men: they are not naturally accorded high status in as many social interactions.

Again, just as you can start looking out for moments in your life when you are being happy high status, you can watch out for and notice it in any group. Who is taking status? Who looks most like a leader? Who looks happy high status? Who inspires you with confidence? How could you present yourself to come across more like them? The more women who can be conscious of this, lift themselves up accordingly, and improve their own performance, the more this bias will turn around. Similarly, the more we can 'give' status to other women when it's appropriate – by observing and praising them, or perhaps by creating a speaking opportunity for them – the better. Can you sit in a meeting and encourage another woman to take the lead? (Be careful not to make this about 'hiding'. It is not about encouraging other women to do the things you're too scared to do.)

Also: let go of the 'woman' thing from time to time and just be you. It can be exhausting to think of yourself the whole time 'as a woman' and to be aware of all the things that women have been up against for a long time. When you speak up and speak out, you are taking on some of those things. But also you need to learn how to let them go and set them aside. You cannot be carrying the entirety of womankind and 'representing' the whole time. Of course, this is a book for women and about women. But I am not suggesting for a moment that women need special help in this area while men don't. Women are just as able to be stellar speakers as men are. And, in some cases, women even have an advantage because in many fields they will still be in the minority: a large part of speaking is about being memorable and standing out. At this stage in history women have an opportunity to do that in a way that men often don't.

Without getting into the realms of conspiracy theory, I do think this is a double-edged sword for women. On the one hand, they have the opportunity to stand out more and be noticed. On the other, they are more likely to be subject to harsh judgement and criticism. Donald Trump, for example, has a pompous, unpleasant, self-congratulatory speaking style and a grating voice. But he is not criticized for these things in the way that Hillary Clinton was criticized for her speaking style and voice.

When I am working with groups of women, I ask them to think about all the different types of male leader and speaker they have encountered. There are hundreds of examples all around us, just in the daily news cycle, from ministers and CEOs to football managers and religious leaders. Of course, there are many examples of women leaders in the news too, but the simple truth is that there are not as many and they are not as prominent. And even if the women are relatively prominent now, that's a recent development. All I'm trying to show is that if you want a role model of a male leader, no matter how eccentric or idiosyncratic or unusual (hello, Trump, again), it's not difficult to find one. With women there are fewer examples. We have hundreds of years of male leadership behind us. We are only just in the first few decades of prominent female leadership. We are only just beginning to see what female leadership – good, bad, ugly, eccentric, electrifyingly brilliant – looks like and how varied it can be. It's up to every woman who wants to lead to find her own style and her way of making her mark.

The ultimate goal should be for you to express yourself as an individual, regardless of your gender. I like to think that, in years to come, there will be many different styles of speaking and leadership, and they will not be divided into 'masculine' or 'feminine'. Just as many of the examples I have given do not fall into precise categories. All of the speakers here have learned to express themselves as individuals, not according to some pre-ordained standard.

Don't forget that women used to be the drummers

Finally, an eccentric but beautiful thought about the bonkers magic of drumming, which has sustained me many times when I've felt down and dispirited about my own speaking. I think something deep inside us believes the horrible, ancient Samuel Johnson quote, that a woman 'preaching' is like a dog walking on its hind legs. There are many unspoken cultural barriers against women speaking and we carry a lot of them unconsciously inside, telling ourselves things like 'I don't have anything important to say' or 'Who am I to speak?' or 'Why should anyone listen to me?' I think most of us recognize that these aren't valid objections. They're just the noise of insecurity and self-doubt.

Instead of focusing on these pointless thoughts, I think instead about a book I came across once while staying with a woman in one of the world's last hippie communes, outside Nashville, Tennessee. (It's a long story. I was inter-viewing a midwife who has helped with hundreds of natural births. She has lived there since the 1970s.) Having gone to bed after a vegan meal of tempeh and beansprouts grown in the soil of the commune, I woke up slightly disoriented. The first thing I saw next to my bed was a book, whose title read: *WHEN THE DRUMMERS WERE WOMEN*. I was intrigued. It turned out to be a meticulously researched history of female drumming by the late woman percussion-ist Layne Redmond. What? I remember thinking sleepily. Since when were the women drummers? But we were. We were the drummers in the ancient world. Men were not allowed to be drummers. This is not a theory that is men-tioned often, and Layne Redmond's book, published in the 1990s, is long since out of print and forgotten. Instead another story is told.

It's a truism often mentioned when people are talking about resistance to public speaking that it goes against our 'tribal instinct'. For hundreds of years, it was dangerous for human beings to be individualistic or to do anything that involved stepping outside the group. The idea of being a 'lone wolf' or an 'isolated individual' supposedly goes against our primitive experience. The feelings of fight-or-flight that kick in when we're in this scenario are some of the few remnants left inside us of the lives our ancestors led. This is why so many people (men and women) struggle with the idea of speaking and why, as Jerry Seinfeld has joked, at a funeral most people would rather be in the coffin than in the pulpit. The rational human mind tells us that we can easily speak in front of a group. (And this is true. We can.) But something else – which we can physically feel and is sometimes intensely painful – tells us it's a very bad idea. Once upon a time, this feeling was strong enough to make sure we would never isolate ourselves from the tribe because otherwise we could die.

Layne Redmond offers a completely different story and it's one women should know about. She writes about prehistoric women (from several thousands of years BC) who were priestesses. They were separate from the people they lived among and acted as leaders by virtue of being brilliant at drumming. They thought of themselves as being descended from the goddesses who first transmitted music to humans: 'For 3,000 years women had been the primary percussionists of the ancient world.' Then, she argues, as Christianity came in, it became sinful for women to practise music. Now, on the most basic level, there was no role for women where they could stand outside the group and lead it in a communal activity. Before, the drumming rituals had been important for meaning and bonding: they were used at times of ritual and celebration.

It's a bit of an ask to get all women to take up drumming and start beating out their rhythm on the bongos to reclaim the sacred rites of the goddess. Maybe when I get really fed up with things, you'll find me in a moonlit clearing, swaying gently and beating a very large tambourine. Until then, I don't think there's anything wrong with channelling the spirit of the women Layne Redmond writes about. You do not need a drum to be heard. You do not need to become a priestess. All you need is a voice and an idea of what you might like to say. No more excuses. Go and own the room.

11

Be More You 2.0:
Video-Conferencing,
Virtual Communication
and How to Own
the Zoom

Owning the room when you're not in the room

How do you 'own' it when you are just a picture on a screen? How on earth are you supposed to maintain your hard-won happy high status when you're trapped in a little digital box that keeps freezing? Whose idea were all these Zoom calls anyway? Believe me, I feel your pain.

This angst is not new. I've been hearing questions about video-conferencing technology for the past five years. Usually from employees of tech and financial companies where platforms like Microsoft Teams or BlueJeans were already being commonly used pre-pandemic to save on travel costs and/or to increase collaboration. Their questions were no different from the ones being raised now that everyone is using such platforms. And, come to think of it, the questions are often no different from the ones most commonly asked in relation to real-life meetings. How do you make yourself heard when one person is dominating? How do you ask a question without being seen to interrupt the speaker? How do you draw out people who are not contributing?

Then there are questions that relate exclusively to on-screen meetings. Where exactly should you look? When – if ever – is it OK to turn your camera off? When should you use the Mute button? How much time is reasonable to spend on screen over the course of a day? I have heard of people spending up to eight to ten hours a day on Zoom. This seems crazy-making to me. After forty-five minutes, I'm personally close to my daily limit. No one loves these meetings and everyone struggles to work out how they could come across better in them. The aim, then, of this chapter is to make this technology feel friendlier, more effective and less irritating. Because whatever we think about it, one thing is certain: it is not going away.

Owning the room when you are not in the room – indeed, when no one is in the same room, because everyone is working from home – is not as recent a thing as you might think. Early experiments in video-conferencing took place in the 1930s. The first commercially packaged option was showcased at the World's Fair in New York in 1968. FaceTime launched in 2010. Google Hangouts arrived in 2013. Zoom was born on 21 April 2011. Arguably, though, it has taken the pandemic of 2020 to force us into using these systems. I'm not sure we use them by choice. Only by necessity. Which is perhaps why they took decades to develop: there was no urgency, and a heightened awareness of their flaws. But now is the time to use them with some degree of gratitude. It seems likely that there will be times in all our futures when they will be the only thing standing between us and the social abyss.

Let me make it clear that when I mention 'owning the Zoom' in this chapter, I'm using the phrase as a catch-all for the dozens of options for on-screen video communication, from GoToMeeting and Cisco Webex to Skype and House-party. The word 'Zoom' has become to screen communication what the word 'Hoover' is to vacuum cleaning and 'Google' is to internet searches. It doesn't matter whether you're using Zoom or not, it's what people have started to call screen communication.

The point is, whatever we call this activity, Zoom is now part of our lives. This chapter doesn't aim to discuss the merits of different methods of screen communication, but looks instead at what they all have in common: the ability to showcase you remotely in your best light. What are the basic rules that will allow you to achieve that, no matter what platform you're on?

'But I hate Zoom, and I just don't want to use it'

I'm sorry to say it, but I'm afraid this is like saying, 'I hate using the phone,' or 'I hate using email,' or 'I want a job, but I don't want to do any actual work.' Some of us do hate the phone and email. And lots of us definitely want to get paid for doing no work. But we have to find a way around these feelings in order to get by. It's going to be the same with Zoom and all the rest. Embrace the inevitability.

When it comes to hating video-conferencing technology, the thing is that it doesn't care what you think about it. Zoom doesn't care that it's no match for being in the same room as someone, being able to read their body language, and feeling the comforts and risks of real eye contact. We waste time and energy by being angry with or disappointed by these platforms. Of course they have limitations. Of course they're not as good as being with real people in a real room with real air to breathe and real awareness of who is giving the boss the side-eye. But here's the thing. There are going to be times when they are the best available option. Not necessarily the best option. But the best *available* option.

I feel passionate about our acceptance – even our embrace – of these systems. The sooner we learn to do more than tolerate them, the better. We need to master them, enjoy them, put them at our service, in the same way that we have with phones and social media. To be blunt – and please turn away if you are of a sensitive disposition – we need to make Zoom our bitch.

Why is this so important? Because our emotional burden is being constantly weighed down in modern life. Not only when our countries are in lockdown or suffering the consequences of a pandemic or another crisis. Even when we are not in crisis, our emotional bandwidth – our capacity to connect and focus – is taxed by the multiple demands of home life, work, financial pressures, trying to stay healthy . . . At all times, whether good or bad, there are multiple factors that exert stress upon us. So why let screen technology be an extra stressor? Why waste time and energy on hating Zoom if it's the best available option – and, let's face it, an inevitability? The best thing to do is adopt a neutral attitude towards it and think, 'I don't have to fall in love with this thing. But I'm damned if I'm going to be broken by it.' Who knows, you might surprise yourself.

No one knows what they're doing on video-conferencing (except, perhaps, newsreaders)

No one is using these platforms perfectly. No one can claim they're an expert. Our use of them is in its infancy. In June 2020, on a conference call with Wall Street to announce the company's latest earnings, Zoom founder and CEO Eric Yuan forgot to unmute himself at a critical moment, leading to confusion amongst key investors. The previous week his personal stock in the company was valued at above $10 billion. He laughed off the mishap. So please don't go beating yourself up over rookie errors. Eric Yuan certainly isn't. It's more important to feel confident – and to be forgiving of yourself and to maintain your sense of humour – than to feel that you are fully in control of this technology and how you're perceived on it. Feeling at ease, releasing any feelings of intimidation, being able to improvise, losing your self-consciousness . . . these are a huge part of owning the Zoom.

There is no Academy of Video-Conferencing Performance or Zoom Hall of Fame. As you might imagine with a form of technology that has only been mainstream for the past ten years, there is a real lack of academic and scientific research into the best ways to perform brilliantly whilst using video-conferencing. We can only guess what is working well, and learn from experience. This is a good and a bad thing. It's a bad thing because there is no proven blueprint for effective use. Yes, of course, you can follow the user guidelines. You can google 'change my background on Zoom'. You can learn how to switch breezily between Speaker View and Gallery View. And you can learn to harness a fast finger for the Mute button when your sixteen-year-old starts taking a power shower in the bathroom next door. (This just happened to me on an important call.) The lack of research is problematic, because we have no guidelines governing the 'soft skills' needed for using on-screen apps. But it is also inspiring, because it opens up a space. We can draw our own conclusions using common sense and experience and by swapping notes with other users. We can experiment, and we can fail a little, because time is on our side.

Am I going to cover practical things here like keyboard shortcuts, on-screen features and other hacks? Definitely not. This technology is moving fast and is constantly being upgraded. Practical advice dates quickly. The best way to keep up to speed on individual features, privacy issues, annotation tools, screen sharing or breakout rooms is to google your question or go to the FAQ on the website of your video-conferencing app. If in doubt: go to the source.

But the main reason why I haven't engaged in this kind of practical level of 'expertise' is because I want to demystify these systems. It's not about an expert telling you how best to use them and obsessing about a platform's individual features. It's about you learning to trust yourself and learning by observed example. You will have your own instincts about how you want to come across: be true to them. You may end up developing an on-screen persona that is bolder or quieter than you would be in a face-to-face meeting. That's OK. This technology is not a simulation of real life. But it 'reads' authenticity, level of comfort, confidence and ease in exactly the same way a television camera 'reads' them. As human beings, we see all these things at a glance, even from a very grainy image. We would all be better off putting more work into looking comfortable, relaxed and at ease on camera – just as we would do if we appeared regularly on television – than mastering the technical details of a platform. Work out what you need in order to be secure and to trust in yourself to do the best job that you can, even if you're new to this or struggling. Show up as open, honest and engaged.

Don't look at the screen – look into the camera

First, make sure your camera (usually a pinhole at the top of your screen) is in the right place. It needs to be on a level with your eye line. This will probably mean perching your laptop on a stack of books or using an iPad or iPhone stand. Raise the camera slightly higher than your eyeline and now tilt it forwards. (This should look more flattering.) Make sure you are well lit by ensuring light is falling on your face and never coming from behind you. Now look into the camera. And I mean into it. Really look. This is the first and most important rule of video-conferencing. Perhaps the only rule. It's also the thing that feels the weirdest and the least intuitive.

Looking into the camera feels strange because you are not 'looking' at anyone or anything. You are directing your attention, your gaze and your presence into a tiny circular void. And there will be so many other things that are competing for your attention on that screen: the images of colleagues, the chat function, the collision of audio and video (especially when you are trying to work out who is speaking) and – let us not forget – that most horrific of attention magnets, your own image. Ignore them all. The trick to coming across well to others on screen is to focus on listening, ignore the (distracting and illusory) visual cues and look into the camera. This means blocking out every-thing else. Some people even use a piece of paper or a folded-over newspaper to block out their entire screen so they can focus directly on the camera.

Think about how video works on us psychologically. Can you imagine engaging with the news on television if the newsreader was not looking at the camera? You would immediately change channels. This is why autocue was developed. We care if someone is not looking at us. We care if they look down at a script, because the moment they look down, they lose their focus on us. Even when someone is not talking, we like them to make eye contact with us to indicate that they are listening and engaging. When they don't do this, we think they're not interested. This process of looking at the camera rather than the screen is counter-intuitive, not least because you could ask, 'But if everyone is looking at the camera, then who is looking at the screen?' Which is a good question. But the bottom line is this: the more often you look into the camera, the better you will come across to others when they glance at your face. In reality, if no one looks at the screen and we all look at the camera, it will lead to better interaction anyway, because people will be really listening to what others are saying and won't be distracted by unhelpful and incomplete visual clues.

This is incredibly difficult (but worthwhile) when using video-conferencing platforms. It's a lot of work to keep gazing one-sidedly into that pinhole with no feedback from another human face. But I would argue that it is absolutely worth it. When other people 'look' at you, they will be able to see that you are engaged and listening. And when you are talking, they will be able to see that you are talking to them and with them in mind. If you don't believe that this is as important as I'm making it out to be, then please do an experiment with a friend where you talk to the camera and then talk to different parts of the screen or to your own reflection. You'll soon see the difference. Is it a career-breaking difference? Hard to say. After all, we're all making a lot of allowances for each other at the moment when we're communicating on screen. But does it make a subtle difference in terms of professionalism and persuading others to listen to you – and to believe that you are listening to them? Yes, I really think so. Try it for yourself and see.

The trick is to pretend that you are on television. Because – and this is the problem with video-conferencing, I'm sorry to say – you are on television without actually being on television. Everyone who is watching you will be processing your image as if you are on TV. So be 'on'. Be animated. Have an engaged, 'active listening' expression on your face. I know some of you will be reading this and thinking, 'But, Viv, this is not realistic for the seven hours of Zoom that I am required to do all day, every day.' And you would be right. That is why there are absolutely no television programmes that use the same format as video-conferencing and there never will be. They would be boring and everyone would switch off.

There is a very important lesson there. This technology is most effective when it is used sparingly and carefully curated. There should be a moderator who makes it clear what the aim of the session is. The session should have a clear beginning, middle and end. It should take place within the minimum amount of time possible, not the maximum. Everyone who needs to speak should speak, and ideally should be timed. There are various ways to do this. Appoint a moderator/chair. Appoint a time-keeper. Use break-out rooms. Police the attendance of the meeting. Are there people there who don't really need to be there? Get them off the call. If you are finding yourself in meetings where you can no longer make eye contact with the camera because you've been there too long and you're exhausted, that's a sign: this meeting has gone on too long. Or you are attending too many meetings. I hear a lot of questions about Zoom where the answer is: 'That meeting shouldn't actually be happening.' Or 'You didn't actually need to be in that meeting.' Or 'No one in this company should be on Zoom for more than three hours a day.'

How to make yourself heard and get a point across on screen

Be aware of your purpose in an on-screen meeting. What is the point of your presence? Are you there to contribute or to listen? Your intention should never be 'How can I dominate this Zoom call?' It's more useful to think, 'How can I be useful here? What is the point of me being here? What is the nature of my participation?' You might be there to impart insights, to be entertaining, to offer reassurance or to cut through complicated ideas. Or you might be there to make up the numbers or to offer support. Know the difference. You do not have to 'own' every single meeting. Understanding your role helps you to judge how engaged to look and whether you could turn off your camera for a while and just listen in, whilst checking other work. If you are thinking, 'I have no idea what my role is in any of these meetings or what is expected from me,' then that is a conversation you need to have with the people who are asking you to attend. That is on them, not on you.

If you are an active participant, the key to being heard and getting a point across is to respect the rhythm of the video-conferencing platform and put some thought into how communication flows. On most platforms, two audio streams cannot be heard at the same time. You'll notice this if you're unmuted and you cough loudly or a door squeaks in the background. Instantly the Speaker View (actually Speaker Audio) will transfer to you, even if you didn't mean to make this contribution. This is the other interesting, counter-intuitive thing about these platforms. They appear to be video-based – but actually the technology follows the audio, not the video. It can't 'see' you. But it can 'hear' you.

To be heard, make use of this. When you have an interjection, an interruption or a contribution, make it distinctly. Don't expect it to be an aside and don't wait for permission. In that moment you will cut off the other person and it will be your turn. This feels weird to us, because it's not how usual communication works. In real life, often there's a lull after someone finishes talking and we use visual and audio cues to form a consensus about who is going to speak next. In real life you can cut someone off subtly by talking over them without quite cutting off their point. On Zoom this is impossible: once you cut in, you are the only person who can be heard. So you need to be much more decisive and clear about your interjection. This can feel rude and 'interrupty', but it's just the rhythm of the platform. A good moderator really helps with this. 'Thank you, Kelly. Let's go to Monica.' But without a moderator, you're going to have to be blunt. Dive into your point if you are confident. Or use a bridge: 'Thank you. That was a great point. I'd like to add this . . . ', 'Let me interject here . . . ', 'There's something we really need to be aware of in this context . . . '. If no one is managing to do this on a regular basis and someone is always monopolizing and giving unsolicited monologues, you need to have an off-screen conversation about whether a moderator or a time-keeper is needed. I see too many people (especially women) thinking it's their job to fix this almost unfixable problem in the moment. Without any guidelines or framework, of course someone will be tempted to turn it into a one-person webinar.

What if you like banter or making remarks under your breath that are not really relevant to what's being discussed? (This is me, basically.) I'm afraid you need to learn to shut up. These interjections, which are often calming or refreshing in real-life meetings, can be extraordinarily disruptive and unhelpful when you're using on-screen technology. In some contexts that's what Chat is for, provided you're in an environment where Chat is welcome or encouraged.

The difference between work and downtime on screen

There is a gigantic difference between your use of this technology for work reasons and your use of it in your free time. If you are talking with your boss on Zoom, it is not the same as having cocktails on Houseparty with your friends or talking on FaceTime with your mum. Why? Because of stakes and boundaries. We don't often talk about these things or acknowledge them, but they're there the whole time. If I'm on a FaceTime call with my sister, it doesn't matter if neither of us looks into the camera. She is not going to think any less of me and our relationship is not going to suffer as a result, however many times she has a conversation with my chin.

The question is this: 'To what degree is professionalism required in this situation?' Clearly you do not need to display professionalism if you are talking to your family or friends. Work situations, however, are another matter. There's a very good reason to present yourself on screen in exactly the same way that you would in real life: self-respect. It doesn't really matter if all your colleagues turn up looking under-dressed, bored and indifferent. That is their standard. Let yours be higher. It may not reflect how you are feeling inside (and you may well be feeling bored and indifferent). But if you do the professional equivalent of getting out of bed, brushing your teeth, giving yourself a good scrub and putting a brave face on, this has psychological consequences both in terms of how you perceive yourself (which will affect your presence and performance) and in terms of how others perceive you.

This doesn't necessarily mean that you always need a full face of TV-ready make-up and blow-dried hair. Although by all means do that if it makes you feel good and feel like 'you'. But it does mean that you have to put some thought in. Do I look presentable and professional? Would I be OK with doing a job interview looking like this? Would I upload myself to YouTube looking like this? Would I do a slot for a TV show looking like this? Because, as I've said already (and can't say enough), whether you like it or not, that is how it 'reads' when you are on screen. Unless we are in very relaxed, low-key social situations with friends using screens, we don't have a part of our work brain that says, 'Oh, I'll give Janet a break today because we're only on Zoom and it's not that important a meeting.' Our brain goes straight to this thought: 'Janet isn't into this meeting. She might as well not be here. Is that a hat? Or is that her hair?' Don't be Janet.

Tips and Tricks

— The only real way we are going to get comfortable about using this technology is by sharing information and insights. Ask friends and colleagues: 'What is working for you here? What is not working?' 'Do you know anyone who comes across really well on this app? What do they do differently to other people?'

— Take pictures with your phone or screenshot yourself while you're on screen. (You can screenshot yourself on most keyboards using Shift Command 4. Or google 'screenshot capture' for your device.) This is the equivalent of someone taking pictures of you while you're at an event. You can see how you come across to the 'audience'. You can also do a test call. Ask a friend to take pictures of you on screen looking in different places: looking at your own image, looking at an image low down on the screen, looking directly into the camera. In my view, we should all aim to look directly into the camera as often as we can bear it. We look brighter, more engaged, more present. To look away from the camera is the equivalent of staring at your feet in a face-to-face meeting. You might be listening, but you don't look as if you're really 'there'.

— Make sure a light source is shining on to your face and not from behind you. Professional broadcasters and social media influencers use 'ring lights' to achieve the best lighting on their face. These are not difficult to acquire: 'ring lights' yields 1.5 billion Google results. If you're in daylight, make sure all the lights in the room are on and that any light from the windows is shining directly on to you. The worst thing you can do is to sit with your back to the window. At dusk or at night, close all the curtains (so that the light doesn't change during the course of your meeting), turn on all the lights and, ideally, shine an additional light on your face. An Anglepoise lamp is great for this. If you have FaceTime on your laptop, you can check the effect in advance simply by opening FaceTime on your screen.

— Do you need to wear make-up or a special outfit? This is such a subjective question. Here's a better one: Would you be comfortable looking like this if you were being filmed for TV or YouTube? I'd love to say, 'It doesn't matter what you look like, it's only a Zoom call.' But we all know that's not true. It matters what you look like in a real-life meeting or a job interview. And even though you're only on screen, you're still at work. Any television presenter will tell you that bright colours, great lighting and basic grooming help. If in doubt, seek the advice of a kind but honest colleague about how you're coming across.

Exercises

— Give yourself thirty minutes a week to research the platform you're using the most. What are people saying about it online? What are the latest hacks and tips? If you feel very nervous and irritated around screen technology, force yourself to watch a 'user's guide' video, either on the website of the company in question or on YouTube. These usually only last a few minutes and are miraculously reassuring. You could also set up a test call, using a personal account – most of these apps have a free version of their service (even if the one you use professionally is a paid-for version). Do a test call with a friend or colleague and practise pushing every button and every option on the screen so that you can see what they do. Try to 'crash' the call on purpose so that you can see how easy it is to get back into it.

— Keep a list of 'interjections' that remind you how to start a sentence when you want to make a point. 'Let me make a point here . . . ', 'There's something I'd like to add . . . ', 'What I'd really like to see us discuss in connection with that last point is . . . '. All these phrases are assertive without being aggressive, and allow the audio time to move to you before you've made your point. They focus the attention gently but firmly on you, whilst buying you a few seconds before you dive in. They are more useful than tentative interruptions like, 'Er, excuse me . . . ', 'Could I just add . . . ', 'Er, can everyone hear me . . . ?'

— If you have to present on a video-conferencing plat-form, practise on your own or with a friend whilst looking directly into the camera. Ideally you should be able to remember most of your key points without having to look down or read anything. But if you do need to read or you need a 'cheat sheet', practise with a piece of paper held level with the camera. I use a shoe box perched vertically, with key points on a piece of paper fixed to the box with Blu Tack. That keeps my eyesight level with the camera. If I were more organized, I'd buy one of those recipe-book-holder things, and perch it on a stack of books to raise it up. Practise imagining the people you are talking to. Remind yourself to smile more than you think is normal. Or, at the very least, keep a smile in your eyes.

— Listen to the episode 'How to Own the Zoom' on Series 7 of the podcast *How to Own the Room* (available free on all podcast platforms). This features lots of practical questions from listeners on everything from meeting etiquette and shutting down 'monopolizers' to how to frame a question and how to prepare ahead.

Appendix

The dos and don'ts of owning the room

My dream for you is not that you will read this book and imagine in your head what your speaking style could be like. My dream is that you will discover your speaking style by speaking. There is only one hurdle: creating the opportunities. Once you have accepted that you are going to do this, it's not as bad as it sounds. You just have to do it.

— Don't make assumptions about speaking before you have much experience of it. (Don't assume something is scary until you've tried it several times yourself. Maybe it's scary for others and not for you – how do you know until you've tried it?)

— Do watch TED Talks and YouTube speeches as much as you can. Find favourite speakers. Work out what you like about them, and what annoys you about the speakers you like less.

— Don't watch these talks and despair. Some of those speakers are stage-managed, produced and rehearsed to within an inch of their lives. Use them for inspiration, not to beat yourself up.

— Do find a speaker whose style closely mirrors what you'd aspire to.

— Don't get caught in dreams of speeches you will never give, such as an Oscars acceptance speech. Unless that really fires you up. Dream about the talks you could give.

— Do start a list of the speeches you could give in the next six months. Are you invited to a wedding? Could you give a vote of thanks to the bride's mother? (I'm not joking.) Do you have a family anniversary or birthday? You can say a few words. What are the work opportunities? Where can you put yourself forward?

— Don't make excuses about why you couldn't possibly make a speech in the next twelve months. You'll be at something this week where you could make a speech if you really wanted to. Start seeing these opportunities.

— Do have three titles in mind for TED Talks – these should cover areas of expertise or passion – or the titles of books you might write if you had time.

— Don't be put off by one bad experience. Or several bad experiences. We all have bad gigs. We all have bad days. We all get caught in situations where no one would have been able to give a good performance. Write down what you've learned and move on.

— Do look for opportunities where you can practise different speaking: off the cuff and improvised; structured and prepared; formal and informal.

— Don't miss an opportunity to tell people you work with that you're looking for speaking opportunities: keynotes, votes of thanks, facilitating, hosting, introducing. But don't wait for others to create them for you. You don't need their permission.

— Do study women in similar roles to yours at work. How do they lead? What do they do when they speak publicly? And watch women in media positions either in your field or whose style you aspire to. How do they project authority? What topics do they talk about? What can you do that is similar to what they do?

Cheat sheet: once you are in the room

Last-minute cheats and reminders for when you are about to speak or go on stage, whether the event is big or small:

— Do a sound check, if you can. Never refuse one. Find out what the back-up system is in case there are any technical issues. Who will you look to if things go wrong? Do you wait for them to find you a back-up microphone? Or is it appropriate for you to continue meanwhile without one? (This is only going to work in a small room.)

— Where is your water going to be if you need it on stage? If you're speaking for longer than five minutes, build in a moment when you'll drink.

— Breathe. Shoulders back. Breathe through the soles of your feet (again, it's a thing). Remember to send your brain to your stomach.

— If it's appropriate – and, unless you're at a funeral, it is appropriate – smile. Smile more than you think is normal.

— If you can feel your nerves as you start, use some time to breathe and take in the room. Breathe. Smile. Feel your feet on the floor.

— If you're not reading from a text, have an idea of your structure. What is your last sentence going to be?

— If you're improvising, have some rules. Hit a precise time target (two minutes, for example) and be strict with yourself. Or promise yourself you'll say ten sentences, then sit down.

— If you have five minutes in which to speak, speak for anything between four minutes and just under five minutes. It's always best to leave people wanting more than to use all your time or run over. If you've said what you want to say in three minutes, made them laugh, think, and have said something that sounds like a strong closing statement, get off.

— Say a definite 'Thank you' as you finish. Then the audience has a clear sign to applaud.

— If you mess up, smile and laugh. Just keep going. It doesn't mean a thing other than that you're a human being and human beings make mistakes. If anything, the audience will like you better for it. Don't dwell on it or berate yourself.

— Finish strong. Be direct with the audience. If you feel it helps, use a signifier: 'And to conclude . . .'; 'I'd like to finish by . . .'; 'I'll end in a moment . . .'

— Walk off calmly and confidently. Now go and plan your next speaking opportunity. (Also: did you video this? You should have done. And you should share it on social media.)

FAQs

— *Even after reading all this, I still feel completely nervous and sick about the idea of speaking. But I need to do it for work. What can I do?* For people who have serious long-term issues and physical symptoms (uncontrollable shaking, sweating, vomiting), I would suggest a workshop on speaking or presenting where you can practise on a very small scale with supportive, trained instructors. I've seen this work very well – and very quickly. Sometimes one attempt at speaking in front of a small group, with the right support, is enough to show people it won't kill them – and that the fear is bigger than doing the thing itself. It's also worth thinking about hypnosis, meditation or mindfulness training. I believe anyone can overcome their fear and become a good speaker. If you think you may have deeper issues around anxiety, it's certainly worth exploring this with your GP or a therapist. See www.welldoing.org for recommendations of therapists.

— *What are the basic rules for facilitating an event?* If you are the host or interviewer, it's important to remember that you're there for the other guests, to make them look good. You are also there as the audience proxy: to make sure they know and understand the format of the event and who the speakers are, and to ask questions on their behalf. Presence is the big rule for this role. You need to listen carefully all the time and experience what the audience is experiencing. If you are thinking about your next question, you may miss something. Ideally be so well prepared that you don't work from notes. No one cares about your notes and what you planned to say or ask. They care about what is happening in the room at the time. My other golden rule for interviewing or hosting is to know as much as possible in advance (about the event and the speakers) but wear that knowledge lightly and invisibly. No one wants a big song and dance about how well prepared you are. They assume that you are. (My pet hate is author events where the interviewer says, 'On page fifty-seven, you introduce a character, blah-blah . . .' The audience hasn't yet read the book. They don't care about page fifty-seven.)

— *How should I handle audience questions at an event?* Know what the plan is and signpost it for your audience if no one else has already done so. Finish your talk with 'Thank you', let people applaud and then say, 'I'll now take audience questions for twenty minutes.' Obviously if there's a facilitator, let them do this for you. If you're taking questions yourself and people are raising their hands, try to cover the whole room (don't take all the questions from the same group of people sitting together). Try to choose a broad mix in terms of gender, age and diversity. If you see a huge sea of hands because so many people want to ask questions, say: 'I see there are a lot of questions. Great. I'll take one-sentence questions three at a time.' Make a quick note of the questions. Keep your answers straightforward and honest. (You're allowed to say, 'I don't know' or 'Thanks – I'll take that as a comment not a question,' if it is not clearly a question.) Answer the questions as best you can and don't be surprised if people ask questions you answered in your talk. Be careful as you come to the end of the time: it can be tempting to take 'one more question' and that question ends up being an annoying person who wants to tell their life story. It's better to finish a minute early than run over. (Again, this is the facilitator's problem if you have a facilitator.) If in the last five minutes of the event you get a great question that gets a big laugh, or you say something that gets a big laugh or a round of applause – or causes a particular moment of recognition in the room – make sure you end the event there and then. 'And with that, I'm afraid we're out of time . . .'

— *I struggle with phone calls and some face-to-face conversations. What can I do?* First of all, recognize that everyone has days when they just don't want to talk to others or have certain phone conversations. Give yourself a break. Occasional low-level anxiety about talking on the phone, having to attend a meeting or facing people when you're feeling low . . . That is all normal. On the phone, standing up helps, especially if it's a difficult conversation or you're trying to get something out of the other person. Follow the breathing advice found on p. 23 before you start: centre yourself, brain in stomach, breathe through your feet. If you're getting really stressed, then do a few minutes on a meditation app to calm yourself. Face to face, the same advice applies; maybe try some power posing in a private place ahead of the meeting (see p. 54). This is highly recommended in particular for job interviews. During the conversation, stay focused and present. Listen. Try not to disappear into yourself and have some empathy for the other person (however annoying they are). What if they've had a bad day? What if they just had some bad personal news? We are all carrying secret worries, even the most egotistical and irritating of people. Focusing on them instead of on yourself is one way of alleviating anxiety.

A guide to creating speaking opportunities

— *Make your own luck.* Just as speakers are made not born, speaking opportunities don't just land in your lap: you need to create and cultivate them. Start small at social events. Propose a toast. Give a vote of thanks. Offer congratulations. Get used to silencing a room and having everyone turn to look at you.

— *To want to do it is enough of a reason to do it.* If you're still thinking, But, Viv, no one has asked me to do this. Who am I to speak? I would reply yet again until it gets through: 'Who are you not to?' No one wants you to stand up and give a twenty-minute speech at the school fair. But if you're at an event where you can clear your throat, clink your glass with a fork and say, 'I'd just like to say . . . thank you to the committee for creating a fantastic event. We're all really grateful to you for your hard work. Let's raise a glass . . . to the committee!' That will take ten seconds out of people's lives and you will have made the committee (or whoever it may be) feel special.

— *Experiment at work.* Once you've done a couple of social-event speeches, think about work opportunities. Yes, talk to colleagues and managers and put yourself forward so that people know you want to speak. But also think about what you can do yourself. Can you create a half-day event? Or even a half-hour event? I have hosted events where everyone who wants to can get up and speak but for no more than two minutes. It's run like an open-mic comedy night. It needs someone to host and move things along. Anyone can speak, but they're strictly timed (and they don't have to use their entire two minutes). They can talk about whatever they want: a story, a poem they know by heart, some jokes, a few words on a cause they're passionate about. The whole point is that no one has prepared for it. If you can get twenty people in a room, you've got an event. It's a great icebreaker or finale for corporate events.

— *Prove yourself first.* There's nothing more annoying at work than someone who keeps saying, 'I want more speaker opportunities,' but is not doing anything about it. Make it easy for people to think of you and choose you. Be the one who is creating opportunities for others as well as for yourself. If you work from the premise that no one else is going to do any of this for you, you can't be disappointed – and you can only be surprised by other people's generosity if something does land in your lap.

— *Make your intentions clear on social media.* The more video content you have on your social media, the more obvious it is to others that you are comfortable with speaking.

— *Hone your skills.* Think about taking a workshop on improvisation, stand-up comedy, presentation, speaking or facilitating. Google is your friend. In London I recommend Spontaneity Shop, the FA, Logan Murray and How to Academy.

— *It's not just about TED but . . .* I have met many people who say that it is their dream to do a TED Talk. This makes me laugh as I will then say, 'That's great. What would your title be?' And they don't have a title or a subject. If you have neither, you have no TED Talk. Unless you're willing to reach out and propose a title or a subject, you have no TED Talk. Also, if you have no video of yourself giving a talk, you have no TED Talk. (You need a video for your application.) It's important in life to recognize what is a dream and what is a fantasy. If you want to do a TED Talk, no one is stopping you doing one.

In order to speak at TED, you have to apply. You can nominate yourself (or anyone) for an eighteen-minute talk on the Speaker Nomination Form on the TED website (http://speaker-nominations.ted.com). You need to include your title and subject area and include a video of yourself speaking. (This might be a time to look at the ideas you wrote down for one of the exercises at the end of Chapter 3, page 70.) My advice for anyone who is serious about this would be to find a TEDx first. TEDx events happen locally so you can google 'TEDx' plus the name of anywhere you could get to. Or type: 'TEDx event speaker application'. Most have submission forms or contact emails. In my view, the odds of being chosen for this are higher than of being chosen for TED.

— The more speaker experience you get, the clearer you will become about your subject matter. Ideas for developing this: What is your passion? What is the change you want to see in the world? What do you know most about? Have you been through an experience most people haven't? What do you find easy to do that other people find difficult? What's the one thing in your industry you would love to see change? What makes you angry? What inspires you? These are all things people would like to hear a speech about.

— Before you do TED, or to get your TED application video, here are some places where you could offer to speak:
  • At your old school or anywhere you've studied.
  • Anywhere that a teacher who taught you works. Teachers will always be happy to miss a class to have someone from the outside come in and speak.
  • At the school of any friend who is a teacher. What teacher doesn't want a lesson off?

- The Women's Institute has regular speaker slots on a huge variety of topics from gardening and interiors to careers and science. (If you're thinking, But, Viv, my dream is not to talk to the WI, it's to do a TED Talk, then I can guarantee that your TED Talk will be a hundred times better if you've performed it to half a dozen Women's Institute groups first. It was not my dream to perform for the WI (sorry, WI), but I wouldn't have known how to put together an Edinburgh show if I hadn't done about ten previews a year for WI groups up and down the country three years running.)
- Somewhere you used to work. Ask a colleague: 'If I came back, what would be useful to hear from me?'
- Somewhere you want to work. 'I have a twenty-minute talk about the new development in our industry that everyone is talking about. Can I come in and talk to a group of your people?'

Further reading

These are all books that have helped me with speaking. Some are about personal development: 99 per cent of speaking is how you feel about yourself and whether you're comfortable getting up in public to show people who you are. That is the work of a lifetime. Some are more technical and some are about others sharing what has worked – and not worked – for them.

— Brené Brown, *Daring Greatly: How the Courage to be Vulnerable Transforms the Way We Live, Love, Parent and Lead* (Penguin, 2013). An excellent meditation on courage and what it means to open up. A great addition to her TED Talks.

— Susan Cain, *Quiet: The Power of Introverts in a World that Can't Stop Talking* (Penguin, 2013). This is the Bible for anyone who thinks, But I'm too shy to speak. You don't have to be loud and outgoing to be a good speaker. You can be a quiet and private person. Cain's argument is that we are losing out on a lot of valuable contributions because we buy into the myth that extroverts are the best speakers.

— Amy Cuddy, *Presence: Bringing Your Boldest Self to Your Biggest Challenges* (Orion, 2016). A great guide to body language and how the way you present externally influences not only how other people perceive you but how you perceive yourself. The ideal reminder to avoid hunching and to stand tall.

— Tim Ferriss, *Tribe of Mentors: Short Life Advice from the Best in the World* (Vermilion, 2017). The author is the alpha male of the self-transformation world, and here he gathers everyone he has ever interviewed for his podcasts and extracts their nuggets of wisdom about excellence, productivity, motivation and, of course, speaking.

— Caroline Goyder, *Gravitas: Communicate with Confidence, Influence and Authority* (Vermilion, 2014). Goyder is a brilliant performance and voice coach, and a great speaker. In this book she explains how we can each access our own natural gravitas. Superb advice on persuasion and influence.

— Tara Mohr, *Playing Big: A Practical Guide for Brilliant Women Like You* (Arrow, 2015). Don't be put off by the title. This is my favourite book on women and career by a coach who has nailed every limiting belief we struggle with. From working with your inner critic to getting advice from your future self, this is an incredibly inspiring and practical read.

— Amy Morin, *13 Things Mentally Strong People Don't Do* (William Morrow, 2014). This book saved me from an intense attack of self-loathing at the Edinburgh Fringe one year. Morin is a psychologist who lost her husband at a young age. Here she talks about her own experiences and those of her clients as she investigates how to fight a negative mindset and build resilience.

— Logan Murray, *Be a Great Stand-Up: Teach Yourself* (Teach Yourself, 2010). On the surface, a how-to guide to stand-up comedy. In reality this is an inspiring and funny read about overcoming performance anxiety and developing material. It has some great exercises that will help anyone generate material for a speech that needs some jokes in it.

— Gretchen Rubin, *Better Than Before: What I Learned About Making and Breaking Habits – to Sleep More, Quit Sugar, Procrastinate Less, and Generally Build a Happier Life* (Two Roads, 2016). Rubin is the expert on changing your habits. If you have got into the habit of avoiding speaking opportunities, thinking you're not good enough or just being a bit lazy, she has dozens of ways to shake you out of it. The ultimate guide to breaking through your own stupid excuses.